FATE'S GAME
AND
OTHER STORIES

FATE'S GAME
AND
OTHER STORIES

Kodagina Gouramma

Translated from the Kannada by Deepa Bhasthi

YODA PRESS
79 Gulmohar Enclave
New Delhi 110 049
www.yodapress.co.in

Translation Copyright © Deepa Bhasthi 2023

The moral rights of the author have been asserted
Database right YODA PRESS (maker)

ISBN 978-93-82579-82-3

Editors in charge: Ishita Gupta and Arpita Das
Typeset in Adobe Minion Pro, 11/14.4
By MSourcing
Published by Arpita Das for YODA PRESS

Contents

Acknowledgments

My thanks and gratitude,

To Gouramma's grandson Ashok Krishna and his family for sharing the author's photos, for their co-operation;

To Mini Krishnan, who over a single phone call gave me the push I needed to get here;

To Ishita Gupta, Arpita Das and the team at Yoda Press;

To Priya Mathew and Bhargavi Kerur, for every conversation about life;

To my parents, Sudha and Prakash, who don't always understand why I do what I do, but support me unconditionally nevertheless.

In the ten years that Gouramma has lived in my head, I've talked about her work with innumerable people. This translation is better for every discussion, every critique, every thumbs up, every feedback from each of them. Of this long list of people, my thanks especially to Dr Taltaje Vasanthakumara, Sajai Jose and Akshaya Pillai, for friendship and kindness.

Most of all, my love to Nan, without whom not much would mean anything.

Translator's Note

Gouramma has lived in my head for a good part of a decade now. It is therefore hard to decide where to begin when I want to introduce her to readers here, tell you how she is important and so on. Thanks to her obscurity even within the cloistered region of her, and my, birth, I only heard of her work via a Sunday newspaper feature a little ahead of her birth centenary year. In my perfect naivety, I had planned to have a translation of her short stories published by the end of 2012, the year she would have turned a hundred. But she had not lived past the prime of her youth, or beyond the very beginning of her writing career. And it was not until many years later that Mrs G started to want to get out of my head again. Now, here we are.

Gouramma, or Kodagina Gouramma—she who was of Kodagu, a tiny southwestern district in Karnataka—or Mrs B. T. G. Krishna as she sometimes liked her name printed with her stories, was born in March 1912. She married B. T. Gopalakrishna, the manager of a large coffee plantation in 1925, became a mother to 'Baby' Vasanth in 1931, the year she also started writing, and died in a swimming accident in the summer of 1939, a month after her 27th birthday. These dates are to be noted while constructing an image of the world and times she lived in, and while reading nuance into the stories of the time of which she wrote.

One of the three major women writers in Kannada in the early 20th century, Gouramma's career was only about eight years and 21 short stories long. In those brief years, apart from inhabiting demanding familial roles of wife, mother, aunty, sister, and so on, she was also a nationalist, a freedom fighter, a budding politician, a tennis enthusiast, an ace swimmer (wearing bikinis in public, in an orthodox village no less, they say), a voracious reader and letter-writer and a polyglot. Her writing career was likely becoming her main focus; for towards the end of the 1930s, she was regularly corresponding with several of her peers, seeking advice and feedback from giants of Kannada literature like Kota Shivarama Karanth, Da Ra Bendre and others who visited Gundukutti Estate, where she lived and her husband worked. She was also attending literary conferences far and near and starting to find her voice.

While looking at Gouramma's literary life, it is tempting to draw parallels with the short lives and productive careers of the Brontë sisters. But that would be doing Gouramma's works a disservice. She is likely to have read plenty of 19th-century English literature, given how easily they were available; maybe she even read the Brontës. Though steeped in the local context of 20th-century life in a remote corner of the country, her writings show an awareness of and an appreciation for literature from elsewhere in the world. A similar outwardly view is limited in the local placemaking and decidedly Victorian concerns of the Brontës. Gouramma's comfort with Western ideas and the English language is unmissable in her stories. It is tempting to speculate what her writing career would have looked like in later decades, influenced by nationalist ideas, her burgeoning feminism and her ability to engage with the outside world.

Hardur, a remote outpost in a village called Suntikoppa where she would move after marriage, was a far cry from the cosmopolitan Madikeri where she was born and raised in a well-to-do upper caste family. Having lost her mother at a very young age, Gouramma was raised by an indulgent father. Her husband was just as progressive. If this were not so, a woman in the 1920s and 1930s would not have found it easy to pursue the varied interests that she did.

Highly influenced by Mohandas Gandhi after having met him during his visit to Kodagu in 1934, Gouramma travelled the district in later months to recruit members for the Congress party. It is interesting to note that she believed in a policy of one national language for one country, as evident in some of her letters, and went on to master Hindi, encouraging her family to learn it too. It is useful here to again remember the times she lived in and the popular sentiments of those years while reading into her politics and some of the ideas she explored in her writing.

Gouramma's twenty-one stories, all included in this collection, can be divided into three wide themes: those related to widowhood and its violence on women, stories of love and heartbreak, and those reflecting on the problems arising from demands for dowry. Her older contemporaries Nanjanagud Tirumalamba and R. Kalyanamma (both widows from a very young age and of similar social circumstances as Gouramma) chose to often reiterate orthodox solutions for women's issues and toed the prevalent societal line of that period in their works. But Gouramma's short stories are uncompromising in their progressive, feminist stand, nearly always seeking a complete overhaul of the status quo in patriarchal society, if women were to be emancipated. She uses her rebellious, confident characters to question patriarchal dogmas, seeking to loosen the knots of empty tradition and religious sentiments that were, and still are, used to suppress women.

Gouramma's stories follow the Navodaya tradition in Kannada literature that had begun to be adopted by writers around the turn of the twentieth century. This period of literary renaissance discarded stories of kings and queens, gods and goddesses, and explored contemporary social issues that were influenced by a complicated mix of modern education and the nationalist movement. Completely devoid of archaic and mythological themes, her women grapple with the demands of love, betrayal and sacrifice while remaining caught in a web of family, tradition and duty. Several focus on the plight and emancipation of widows of all ages. In an author's note attached to her story *Remarriage*, her first story, written in 1931 after the birth of her only son, she mentions an incident that made her partial to writing about widows, in fact, being an inspiration for all her writing, but goes no further in detailing what that incident was. These stories about widows form the bulk of her oeuvre. The rest, while always women-centric, explore love, heartbreak, redemption and betrayal. There are many happy endings as well, though not before subtly questioning the repression, the unreasonable expectations placed on women and the orthodoxy of that time and age. In highlighting the issues affecting women and seeking social reform, her stories remind one of the works of Lalithambika Antarjanam, who was also starting her career in adjoining Kerala in the same period as Gouramma in Kodagu.

While Gouramma's female characters almost always take a strong, and often painful, decision to walk away from a marriage or an ill-fated affair, the men in her stories are portrayed as either helpless, weak-willed and unable to challenge rigid social norms or are shown as perpetrators of injustice. The upheaval in the lives of her women because of lovers, husbands or brothers is often catastrophic. These women do not always have the agency to stand up for themselves. But rarely are they mere victims of circumstances. In the choices they make, they show independence, immense courage and guts far beyond what their age and societal pressures otherwise allows them.

Gouramma's works are strongly embedded in the social circles that were like her own, though she certainly led a much more emancipated life than the women she wrote. Hers was a world of educated, landed gentry who sent their children, though mostly only sons, to Madras and England to study. Her father and a brother were in the law, as were several other members of her extended family. Mirroring a world she would thus have been rather familiar with, the men in many of her stories are often travelling to study law, or practising it. But in spite of education and exposure to a wider world, these sections of society also remained codified by the fragmented and exclusionist world of caste, class, honour, duty and perpetuated the idea of how a 'good girl from a respected family' ought to behave.

Gouramma's characters grapple with conformity and rebellion in ways that transcend specificities and speak to the archetypal struggles of women in a patriarchal society. There are no easy answers, if any at all, to the questions she asks, nor does she offer one-size-fits-all solutions. She chooses not to philosophize and burden her characters with a heavy baggage of morality. Instead, her sentences are simple and almost matter of fact, with little drama and emotion. Her style was thus also modern at least two decades before the Navya movement, which rejected the Romanticism of Navodaya, became popular in Kannada literature. U. R. Ananthamurthy, whose novel *Samskara* is perhaps among the most famous examples of this period in Kannada literary history, would go on to employ similar thematic concerns of caste, and question rigid orthodoxy more openly a few decades later. Gouramma's stories were among the earliest feministic writings in contemporary Kannada literature. Though not extensive, her contribution to literature, and to feminism in literature, is significant for having laid the path down for other women-centric writings by Triveni, Anupama Niranjana, M. K. Indira and Vaidehi in later decades.

A monograph on Gouramma, written by H. Nagaveni and published by the Sahitya Akademi details how a lot of her stories were based on real life incidents, stories of family and distant relatives, of workers in the coffee estate and so on. While some of her stories were published in general interest publications like *Jaya Karnataka, Rashtrabandhu, Prajamatha* and were included in an anthology of short stories by women writers, as collections, *Kambani* (Tears) and *Chiguru* (Bud) were published posthumously in 1939 and 1942, respectively. In later reprints, both these books began to be published in a single volume.

Gouramma was far from being at the height of her writing prowess when she died. However, her maturity in questioning age-old practices and recognizing the quiet strength and resilience of women even in the worst of circumstances is noteworthy. Some of her ideas about the lot of women need to be read in the context of the times she wrote in, but her thematic concerns—patriarchy, caste rigidity, women's emancipation—remain relevant and just as urgent, nearly a hundred years after Gouramma wrote her stories. They are classics and remain fresh, as if they were composed just the other day.

Some Letters

1.

Madikeri,
30 March 1932

Greetings of love to Shriman Vasantha Rao....

It is impossible to hide this from you any longer. I love you. With all the innocence and purity with which a woman can love a man, I love you. What? Is loving a sin? Do others have power over our heart? From the time you were ill and bedridden in Aunty's house and I started taking care of you, I have been in love with you. When I was looking after you, I was the happiest. But I no longer have that good fortune. Your wife arrived yesterday. Aunty and your wife both suspect that something is going on between us. I could not hide the fact that I was in love with you. Can feelings of love ever be hidden? When we live in society, we have to be bound by its ties too. I will go away to my boarding house today. My feet are reluctant to walk away from you in this state. If I stay here, people will unnecessarily doubt us. It is not easy to change the hearts of people. Please do not grieve. I do not have the courage to say these things to you in person, hence I sought to write this letter. Forgive me.

Prabha

2.

Madikeri
30 March 1932,
Evening 4.30

Prabha, I have only fallen sick; but I am not blind. I am aware of your love; I have seen people's suspicions too. Why hesitate over the truth? That you will get a bad reputation for my sake is what saddens me. That my wife also does not trust me is what upsets me. I did not even in my dreams think that she would also suspect me. Anyway…forget all this. Be the way you were earlier. Do not change your behaviour. Don't go. You know very well with what pure feelings I love you. If you leave, I will be much aggrieved.

Vasantha

3.

Madikeri
1.4.32

Prostrated greetings to Shri Vasantha Rao.

To do what you wrote is impossible for an orphan like me, I must bow down to the shackles of society. The good fortune of serving you is over now. I don't have the privilege to even come near you now. So what if I am far away? The pure love I have for you in my heart will never be destroyed. Do not write any more letters to me. If someone sees, it will only give way for suspicion. Do not do something that might cause suspicion and give yourself grief. Loving you always,

Prabha

4.

Madikeri
1.4.32
Evening 4.30

Prabha, when there is no sin in our hearts, should we fear what others say? Be the way you were. It is not possible to keep everyone in society satisfied. Do not stop coming to see me. I will talk to my wife, tell her the truth and clear her doubts. Hoping that you will not reject this request.

Vasantha

5.

Madikeri
1.4.32
Evening 6.30

Salutations to Shri Vasantha Rao

What has happened to you? You are talking like a child! What kind of advice are you giving! Don't you understand the problems others will face if I stay here? You say that you will talk to your wife and make her understand. What do you know of a woman's heart? If I go away now, everyone will be happy. In a few days from now you will go to Mysore. Can I come then? You have no control over your heart. The words coming out of your mouth because of your delirious fever will be misinterpreted by people. There is nothing but trouble if I stay here. It is better that I leave.

Yours,
Prabha

6.

Madikeri

2.4.32

Morning 8.35

Prabha, I received your letter. Don't you know me? Don't go. Why are you giving me grief? I do not have the strength to face all kinds of problems. Stay with me always. If my little sister, who left me and went away many years ago, was with me, would people point fingers? I love you in the same way that I loved my little sister. I beg you to stay with me always.

Vasantha

7.

Madikeri

2.4.32

Morning 10.40

Greetings of love to Shri Vasantha Rao

I am an orphan, a weak woman. It is very difficult to listen to false accusations from people. It is impossible to stay here. I will go away tomorrow morning, for sure. This morning when I came to you, you showed a lot of fear. What will people say? If I don't come to see you, you lose your temper with everyone. Don't you have any clue that people might misunderstand this? I cannot see you before I leave. Do not think that this means my love for you has decreased.

Yours,

Prabha

8.

Madikeri
4.4.32

Prabha, why did you go away without giving me at least a glimpse of you? I got to know that you had left the moment I woke up. Did you decide that you would go away while I was asleep? I cannot understand why. After I heard you had left, I felt that we would not meet again in this lifetime. I cannot understand why you left without letting me see you. Did you think I had any improper thoughts about you, Prabha? I swear on god that all I have is a sinless pure love for you.

The doctor says that I will get well soon. But I know, that my stay on this earth is only for a few more days now. This evening I am leaving for Mysore. Forgive my transgressions. It seems you are angry because of my foolishness.

Your well-wisher,
Vasantha

9.

In Vasantha's diary
12.4.32

I came to Mysore on the 4th. After leaving Madikeri I don't have a wish to live. A man should tolerate everything, but the state that I am in, it is impossible for me to deal with such a harsh pain. Why do I always think of Prabha? Cannot a man love a woman the way he might love another man? Why do people point fingers at a friendship between a man and a woman? What is this? Is this the natural rule in society? Is there sin in everyone's hearts? Do people believe that there cannot exist a pure, lust-less, platonic love between a man and a woman? This has become a riddle for me to solve.

10.

Madikeri
Girls' High School
14.4.32

Prostrated greetings to Shri Vasantha Rao.

It is now exam time in our school. That is why there is a delay in replying to your letter. My heart does not agree to do anything else until I write to you, knowing that you will be looking forward to my letter. It looks like you are very worried about me. Forget this unfortunate girl and gain your health back. What shall I say in reply to your letter? I believe I was right to have come away without seeing you. Even if I left without seeing you, my love for you is unshakeable in my heart. What more shall I write? Keep your heart at peace. Do not exert your body. I understand your agony… But what can I do…?

Yours,
Prabha

11.

Mysore
16.4.32

Greetings to Shrimathi Prabhadevi.

Your letter arrived, but since his health has deteriorated, I have not given him the letter. I wish to say a word to you. You writing letters to him is inappropriate. He is my husband. It is not right to have such letter exchanges with other men. It is not decent for respectable women. If you wish him well, then don't write letters to him from now on.

Hoping this,
Sunithi Vasantha Rao

12.

In Vasantha's diary
18.4.32

I will not live now. It does not seem like I have many days left. Why aren't Prabha's letters coming? No matter how hard I try, I cannot understand what it is that I expect from Prabha. What kind of love? I can say it is not a feeling of inappropriate love. There is no lust; there is no desire to possess; then what kind of love? Who shall I ask? I cannot ask Sunithi because she gets angry when I talk about Prabha. She does not understand my intention. She says that water cannot play with fire. Is pure love between man and woman out of reach? Who shall I ask?

13.

Madikeri
Girls' High School
19.4.32

Greetings to dear sister.

I received your letter dated the 16th. Do not worry. I will follow your wishes to the best of my abilities. What you say is right. Vasantha Rao is your husband. He and I have no relationship. I do not have any right to write letters to him. I beg your forgiveness. I will never again write any letters to him. But with all due respect, I make a request of you. Even if you do not have trust in me, please trust your husband. Do not subject him to grief by having unnecessary suspicions; that is all I can write. Do what you think is best. You are educated, and are capable of understanding things. I am an unintelligent orphan...if it seems right to you, I beg you to write to me about his health.

Seeking your kindness,
Prabha

14.

Mysore
20.4.32

Prabha, why are you not writing letters to me? Are you angry? What have I done to make you angry? This is my last letter to you. The days of my life are over. I have no desire to live on this earth either. My heart is on fire from grief. Sunithi doubts me. Love and doubt cannot be together. I am ready for death. I will welcome it peacefully. Begging your forgiveness is the only thing left to do. What can I give you for looking after me when I was sick? All I can tell you is this. The love I had for you in my heart earlier is still there, it will be there in future too.

Vasantha

15.

Mysore
20.4.32

Respected father, I prostrate at your feet in salutation.

I will not live more than eight or ten days now. Please come here soon. Do not grieve seeing this letter of mine. I do not have any fear of dying. In my brief and ordinary life, I have done nothing that would make me afraid of going in front of my maker; why be afraid then? You must feel happy that I am not afraid of going before god. The problems of life and death were created along with the universe. Will the risen sun not set? Do not grieve for me. You must go meet Prabha Kumari at the Girls' High School and find out news about her before you come.

Your loving son,
Vasantha

16.

Madikeri
Girls' High School
23.4.32

Dear sister, greetings.

Vasantha Rao's letter has come. I have promised you that I will not write to him. He thinks that I am angry with him. What shall I do? I learned from his letter that his illness has worsened. Sister, please have mercy and write to me about his condition. Do not speak to him about things that will give him grief. What shall I do? I pray to god that he recovers soon.

Prabha

17.

Mysore
25.4.32

Dear sister,

Is it possible to know what is god's will? He is under a lot of pain these days. After meeting you, father-in-law told him about you. He faints from weakness sometimes. He calls out your name in his sleep and becomes restless. I do not know what to do.

Your unfortunate sister,
Sunithi

18.

Mysore
2.5.32

Shrimathi Prabhakumari,

You must have received the telegram. Yesterday, at 6 o'clock in the morning, my son Vasantha went to heaven. Before he went, he told me everything. He had wished to see you once. He did not send for you because he thought Sunithi would get hurt. Vasantha's last wish was that the expenses for you to stay where you want to and to study as much as you want to should be taken care of. I, his father, also agree to this.

Seetharama

19.

In the May 3rd issue of *Kodagu* newspaper

A 16-year-old girl named Prabha Kumari, studying at the Convent here, is missing from last night. The girl is an orphan. She was studying in the 6th standard. She was a topper in class. She has written a letter addressed to the head mistress. It says: "Do not look for me, I can look after myself, there is no one to cry for me."

A Picture

Rohini was a very sweet girl, more beautiful than Gowri, Sheela or Chandra. God had also given her a personality befitting her looks. That was why I liked her very much. Since she had to pass by our house on her way to and back from school, I used to see her every day. Once in a while, if I was inside doing some work, she would come in, chat for a little while and then leave. All the flowers that bloomed in our backyard were reserved for her. Apart from her beauty and good manners, the fact that I did not have daughters must be the reason why I loved her so much. She brought out a lot of maternal feelings in me.

Rohini's mother had seven daughters; Rohini was the fourth. Since there were children younger than her in the house, there was no one to give her any special love. Maybe that was why she saw my love for her as a good thing. My son Dinesh also liked her a lot. He might have said no if I asked him for something, but for her he would climb the tree and pick guavas; he would pluck flowers from thorny plants and bring them for her; he would draw things for her. Several times he would fight with her and make her cry as well. People used to see them and teasingly call them husband and wife. But Dinesh had grown up alone without siblings and when I saw his love for her, they used to look like brother and sister to me.

Rohini was fourteen years old at that time. She used to study English in the fourth standard. Though Dinesh was only one year older than her, he was sitting for his matric exams that year. He had a lot to study that year, and did not have the time to run around and play with Rohini. She was also slowly crossing childhood, and had started to understand that she was growing up, and that she couldn't continue playing with boys like she had earlier. Seeing her extraordinary beauty grow every passing day, I was incredibly proud. May god give her a good husband, may she have a happy life—I used to pray in my heart every time I saw her. Her sisters Gowri, Sheela and Chandra were all married and lived with their in-laws. All their families were well-to-do; the husbands were all well-educated. It was our desire that Rohini must get a husband who was better than them.

Her father was a progressive man. He believed that girls had to be educated. The first three daughters had been married off in childhood under pressure from their mother. "What is the hurry? Let her at least study a bit," Rohini's father used to tell his wife every time she forced him to search for a groom. It was not that he did not think about Rohini's wedding. If the right groom came by, and if he allowed Rohini to continue her education after the wedding, then her father would not hesitate to get her married. But he had not found such a groom until then, and Rohini had remained unmarried.

Around this time, Rohini's father got transferred and the family left for another town. We were all very sad to part from Rohini who had become like our own daughter in those four–five years of knowing her. She was also not without grief to be going away from us. The sadness of leaving us seemed to have chased away her joy of going to a new place. Her grief choked her so much when they were leaving that she couldn't even say goodbye properly.

That year Dinesh passed his matriculation. Since our town did not have a college, we had to send him to Madras for further education. Our house had already become empty with Rohini's absence; after Dinesh left, it seemed emptier.

One day merged into the other without a difference, and two years passed. In those two years Dinesh came home twice during his holidays. Upon my request, Rohini's mother sent her to our house a couple of times for a few days. Both times, when returning after the holidays, Dinesh would drop Rohini to her house, stay there for two days and then proceed to Madras.

The third year Dinesh did not come home on vacation. Having gone to see the Jog Falls with some friends, he ended up spending the holidays in their house. That was the year Rohini got married. If Dinesh had known she was getting married, he would certainly have come. But the wedding was fixed in a hurry, and I could not attend due to several unforeseen reasons. I was happy though to get to know that Rohini had got a groom who suited her well in appearance, age and education.

I was, however, heartbroken to read a letter Rohini sent a few days later. Just like those who had attended the wedding had said, her husband was·the only son of wealthy parents. He was equal to Rohini in education, looks and age. In her letter, Rohini had not written that all this was untrue, but…!

Aunty, I got married. Apparently, the one who married me is the only son of wealthy parents. It seems he is going to Europe for further studies next week. His father apparently insisted that he get married before going to ensure that he doesn't fall for the charms of some European beauty. He agreed only because he would not be allowed to go otherwise. I have beauty and charm, they say. My beauty would protect their son it seems, so his father told my father: the boy is good looking, educated, and on top of that until he finishes his Europe trip I don't have to go to his parents' house. So, my education will also go smoothly. What other reasons are needed to get married? Yes, I am married. But I do not have the curiosity to even see who it is that I got married to; and I did not. Maybe he also thinks the same way. My younger sister Chitra said that he did not look at me even once. Anyway, I am married now…

…and so on, Rohini had written.

Rohini was not a little girl anymore. She was sixteen years old. She had the maturity to understand her heart. Then why the dissatisfaction even when she got a suitable husband? More than education, looks, youth and wealth, what was it that she desired? Love? Mad girl, Rohini! But still! Her father was progressive. Couldn't he have asked her opinion before the wedding? While it was possible to bend a mature and grown-up girl to suit circumstances, was it possible to bend her heart? If that was to happen, she should have been married off as a child, just like Gowri, Sheela and Chandra. Now? Was this to be the beginning of Rohini's future life, when we had wanted her to be the happiest of all, I thought. No matter how much I thought about it, I didn't know what advice to give her. Her college had started, so I couldn't call her home for a few days and talk to her. Not knowing what to say, I finally wrote:

My dear Rohi, from your letter, it sounded like you were dissatisfied in your marriage. You are like my own daughter. Just as it is natural for me to wish for Dinesh to be happy, as natural is my desire that the vine of your life grows lustrously and remains adorned with beautiful flowers. Though I couldn't come to your wedding, I had asked those who attended and got to know about your husband. I was happy and proud that my cute Rohi has got the right partner. After reading your letter, I was terribly disturbed. Not because you did not get a good husband. But the fact that even though you got a good husband, some unknown shadow seems to have come between you two and this has made me very sad.

Dear Rohi, your husband is young. He is not short of education, looks or wealth. The feather in the cap is that he is courteous also, I have heard from those who saw him. What more do you expect from a husband? Love? Dear Rohi, don't you know that the foundation of love is marriage? Unlike Westerners, the end of love is not marriage for us. Marriage is only the first step for life's true greatness. Your husband is a good man. Why can't your love grow for him? Only now will your real life start. It is not right to hold on to some unknown reason and sacrifice your future life instead of making it beautiful and happy, even if tremendous efforts are required.

Yes Rohi, like you said, you are married. Now no matter what you do, that won't change. It is a knot that binds till you have life.

See, it can be a knot of thorns too. It can even be the sweet touch of gentle flowers. The heart is the main reason for everything. Look how happy Gowri, Sheela and Chandra are! Look at the faces of their cute little children. Look at their houses filled with peace and contentment. They were also married like you. Did their lives get ruined because of that? Looking at their faces can you say that they are not fortunate?

My Rohi, a last word: my desire is that you shouldn't feel sad reading this. Like I said earlier, I think of you as mine just as Dinesh is mine, and that is the reason I write like this. Dear Rohi, you are educated, may your knowledge attempt to germinate the vine of your life instead of withering it. Instead of enabling wrong assumptions to take birth in you, may it fill your life with contentment and peace. This is my biggest wish. My love and blessings.

From Rohini's reply to my letter, it did not seem like her feelings had changed. Maybe she did not want to hurt me. Her next letters did not have anything about her marriage. That year she did not come to our house during the holidays. I guessed that she must have thought she would have to listen to my lectures if she came.

The next year Dinesh left for Germany. Before he left, he visited Rohini's house too. He did not know anything about Rohini's marriage issues. When he was there, he had asked Rohini, "What Rohi, are your husband's letters arriving? Give me his address, when I go there, I will tell him about you." Rohini's crooked face in response to this had greatly surprised him. When he came home, he told me about this. I had to tell him everything then. He loved Rohini like his little sister and was much aggrieved to hear about her issues.

Another three years passed by. Dinesh had finished his studies and was going to return soon. When Dinesh returned, it was my wish to call Rohini home too. She must have thought the whole marriage issue was now old and it won't come up again, and wrote that she would visit. I was elated that after not visiting for three years, she was finally going to come. Rohini arrived one day before

Dinesh. But Dinesh, instead of arriving the next day, sent a telegram saying that he had missed the bus and that he would come the day after with a friend, which he did.

Though I had written to Dinesh that Rohini was going to visit, he did not know that she would already be there by the time he arrived. His smile, already beaming with the joy of coming home, became wider on seeing her. Before introducing us to his friend, he said, "Look Chander, this is Rohi, my younger sister Rohi." Seeing him give her priority in front of someone new, Rohini's face turned red. Dinesh burst out laughing and teased her, saying, "What Rohi, you lock your blabber mouth if someone new comes by? Where has all your chatter gone?" Though Rohini would have otherwise given him the right answer for this, the presence of Dinesh's friend made her keep quiet.

Though it was the first time that I, Rohi and Dinesh had got together after three years, Rohi and I were a little hesitant to talk uninhibitedly because of Chander. But in one or two days, Chander also became one of us. His courteousness had won us over. Though Rohini was reserved around him in the beginning, within a week, she was talking to him with the same ease that she had with Dinesh.

Chander must have been four or five years older than Dinesh. He had completed his education in England and had travelled around Europe for one year. During his travels in Germany, he became acquainted with Dinesh. Their friendship grew and while returning together on the ship, it grew even stronger. That was why, though Chander's family was eagerly awaiting his return, he could not resist Dinesh's invitation and had agreed to spend two weeks in our house.

This was all Rohi and I knew about Chander from Dinesh. It seems like Chander also thought Rohi was my own daughter. He had no reason to believe otherwise from our behaviour. Our house had been empty for many days but was now full with Rohini, Dinesh and Chander. There was laughter, chatter, debate and chaos. Steeped in all this, we did not realize that two weeks had passed. It was time for Chander to go. That was when I was startled awake from the dream of those two happy weeks.

Amidst our joy and happiness, I had not anticipated that Rohini and Chander had young hearts. I had not found it necessary to think whether the familial feelings of love that Dinesh and Rohini had could possibly be what Chander and Rohini, who had never met each other before, had too.

Having lived in Europe for four–five years, along with the education Chander had internalized their habits and behaviour as well. Rohini was a young, well-bred woman who believed that a marriage without love was no marriage at all. None of us had told Chander that Rohini was married either. Her natural beauty, genteel upbringing and behaviour had touched Chander's heart. Likewise, it hadn't been difficult for his education, courteousness, good looks and simplicity to steal her heart. It was my responsibility to have understood this earlier. What now?

It was only when he got ready to leave and was saying goodbye that I realized the depth of their love. I could tell just by looking at their faces. The blind could see it—that was how clear it was, their love for each other, on their faces.

He went away. She was also to leave in a day or two. In her already clouded life, darkness seemed to seep in further.

That night, after Rohini went to sleep, I said to Dinesh, "Dinesh, it seems like Rohi and Chander are in love with each other; didn't you see both their withered faces when he left today?"

He laughed and said, "Oh Amma, it seems like you are practising psychology also now. You saw their faces and got to know that they are in love with each other, it seems!" pushing my words aside.

Though his dismissing my idea made me wonder if my guess had been wrong, the next instant I felt that I was right. But what could I say to Rohini?

Two days later, Rohini also left. Dinesh went to drop her home. Once he came back, he said, "Amma, Rohi's husband has also returned. The news is that within one month he might come to take Rohi back to his home."

Within another eight days a letter came from Rohini's mother. "You did not come to the wedding. At least now you have to come. Aside from us, Rohi is also waiting for you," it said in the letter. I also wanted to talk to Rohini and give her advice. I prepared to leave. Dinesh also came with me.

I couldn't talk to Rohini in private on the day we got there. The next day, her husband came. In the time that everyone was busy receiving and welcoming his family, I took Rohini, her face all withered, to my room. Just as I was about to talk to her, her younger sister Chitra ran in like a storm, "Akka, Dineshanna's friend Chander has come. He is in Dineshanna's room; you must come, they said. Dineshanna is calling," she said all in one breath and ran away.

Though Rohini's face beamed when she heard this, somehow, I wondered why Chander had come now. I went with her to Dinesh's room. Yes, Chander was really there with Dinesh! Chitra, who had run in before us, was standing at the door and asked, "Akka, don't you know him?"

"Why wouldn't she know him? I introduced him to her in our house," Dinesh said, with a smile.

"Poor things! They never saw each other before this!" the naughty Chitra said sarcastically.

"Don't you know that they were both blind at the wedding hall, Chitra?" Dinesh said and laughed loudly. Chitra said, "Blind bhava, blind akka," and laughed. Rohini and Chander also began to laugh, pushing me down from the tall mountain of surprise I had climbed.

Seeing me struck dumb, Dinesh controlled his laughter and said, "Amma, these lovers apparently never saw each other's faces at their wedding!"

From the way Rohini and Chandrashekhar were looking at each other, it seemed like they were going to rectify that mistake now.

Remarriage

Author's note: This was the very first story I wrote, in 1931. The reason behind writing this story, actually, the root of all my stories, is an episode. If you knew about that, you would perhaps know why I am partial towards stories of widows. Back then I thought this was a wonderful story. When I read it now, it makes me laugh to think of all the feelings I had back then. But still, this was my very first attempt, you see, hence I have a bit of an attachment to it.

Gouramma
14.3.1938

* * *

1.

When my wife Savithri left me and went to heaven, I was thirty-five years old. She was thirty. After losing my companion of fifteen years, I felt that life was just humdrum. I had decided to spend the rest of my life as a widower. I felt that bringing someone else in place of my Savithri was a great sin. I was not short of wealth. That was why, within fifteen days of Savithri's death, letters from fathers of prospective brides began to arrive. Even though I was not interested in remarrying, my old mother wished to get me married again. "How many days can you live like this? Will I always be here? After I die, who will look after you and Kusuma? All these people have written letters saying they will give their daughters to you. Can't you marry one of them?" she would say every day and put pressure on me.

I never gave her any answers. Seeing me silent she would start crying. When she started crying, I would leave the room. One day, after much debate about marriage, I got angry with Amma and left the house. But I did not go far. The river in our village is half a mile away from our house. I started for the river to cool my anger. It was evening. I sat on a sand knoll on the banks of the river and began to think about what Amma had said. I felt that her words were true. "If a house does not have a wife, how will the household function? Who will look after Kusuma? One can employ a maid, but who will make sure they do their work properly?" I thought.

I am only thirty-five years old. No shortage of wealth either, what if I get married? If I find the right girl, I decided that I would get married. When I was thinking this, I heard someone laugh behind me. I turned around and saw two girls. Both were young. They were looking at another girl coming with a pot and laughing. The third girl must have been about fifteen years old. The pot accidentally fell from her hands and this was what had made the little girls laugh. I don't think she noticed me sitting there.

"Laughing, are you? Wait, wait," she said and chased them towards where I sat. Seeing me, all three of them retreated. The elder one blushed from shyness. She took the pot and went away with the girls.

2.

The girl I saw by the river was very graceful. From that day onward, day and night, in my dreams and when I was awake, I saw her beautiful blushing face. No matter how much I thought about Savithri, the very next instant that girl's face would be before my eyes. The girl lived near our house in a rented home with her recently-widowed mother. Owing to poverty, she was still unmarried. It seemed like she attended some school. I started to wait outside our house and look at her go to and come back from school. She must have realised this. She then started to walk by the back of the house. I then began to sit on a guava tree in our backyard to wait for her.

I decided that if I did get remarried, it would only be to her. Three months had passed since Savithri's death. Now I barely thought about her. That girl's name was Raji. I thought of Raji all the time. At such times, even if my child Kusuma said, "carry me, Anna," I would get angry. I waited for my mother to broach the subject of remarriage again. But then, it did not seem like Amma was too enthusiastic about bringing up the subject this time. She seemed to have been hurt by how angry I had become the last time she had talked about it. Finally, one day, she began, "What is it son, won't you listen to me?" and proceeded to give me a long lecture. In the end, she even began to cry.

"Amma, why are you crying? Let it be according to your wishes. But only if it is Raji who lives in that house," I said.

Amma was very happy. The same day she talked to Raji's mother. Happy that she was getting a rich son-in-law, the poor mother promised to give Raji to me.

3.

I did not know what Raji's opinion was; neither did I make the effort to find out. There were still four months to the wedding. I found it very hard to get through those four months. Like always, I would sit on the guava tree and look at Raji go to school. Thinking that I wouldn't get to see her if she stopped going to school after the marriage was fixed, I told Amma, "There are still four months left. So what if she goes to school now? Let her go."

"Okay, you all are so modern these days, do whatever you want," she grumbled and kept quiet.

I would see Raji twice every day from the top of the guava tree. One day she saw me sitting there. From the next day onwards, she started hiding her face with an umbrella when she walked by. I had said, "Let her go to school," thinking that I could at least see her face when she walked by. Now that my desire had turned into disappointment, I was greatly upset. I started to think what else I could plan to do to see her. At last, I had an idea. It was her job to fetch water from the river every day. On the pretext of going for a walk, I began to go to the river. She would come with other girls to fetch water. I would sit behind a tree and watch her. The smiling face that she had when I first saw her at the sand knoll had turned serious now. I was surprised to see such a quick change. "Did she not want to get married to me?" I wondered. But the next instant, I thought that was surely not the case. "I am rich; I am still only thirty-five years old. What is her problem if she gets married to me? Who knows, her mother must have said something; that is why she is like that," I thought.

Raji went back with her friends. I came back home too. Four-five days passed like this. Somehow Raji must have seen me hiding behind the tree; she stopped coming to fetch water too. That day, I returned home disappointed.

4.

"Why is Raji not to be seen?" I began to worry. "It is not because she does not want to get married to me," I consoled myself. "If she gets married to me, will she be short of happiness? I am a rich man. My wealth can fulfil her every desire. When this is the case, she cannot reject me. She is shy. That is why she is doing this. After the wedding, everything will be alright," I told my heart.

There were still three months to the wedding. I did not know how to spend those days. If I picked up a book to read, I would see Raji's face instead of the letters. No matter what I did, time just wouldn't pass. My daughter Kusuma used to go to Raji's house. Kusuma was very fond of Raji. Raji too loved Kusuma a lot. These days Kusuma would not come to me at all.

Once, when I was lost in thoughts of Raji, Kusuma had come and said, "carry me" and I had scolded her. From that day onwards, it was rare for her to come near me. Even though she had played with me all the time earlier, it did not bother me that she did not come near me now. Apart from the thought that I had to see Raji, I did not have any other worries. But how to see Raji? The days began to pass in thinking of ways to see her. No matter how hard I thought, I could not come up with any solution. If she had any brothers, at least I could have gone to her house on the pretext of meeting them. How to go there now? I had no excuse to go at all. While going to school, Raji continued to carry an umbrella to cover her face. She would not come to fetch water either. One day Kusuma had gone to Raji's house. She had not come back even though it was evening. Amma called for the servant to go get her. He was not around. I said I would go bring her back. I was deliriously happy that I finally had an excuse to go there.

5.

It was late evening. From a corner of the closed main door, I could see the light of a lamp inside. I knocked on the door. Raji asked, "Who is it?"

I did not speak. She came and opened the door. She did not recognize me as I was standing in the dark. "Who are you?" she asked.

I was silent. Again, she asked, her voice slightly raised, "Who is it?"

I asked, "Where is Kusuma?"

The moment she heard my voice she went back in. "Kusuma, your father has come to call you, go dear," I could hear her say.

"I won't go," Kusuma said.

"You can come tomorrow, go now, my dear," Raji said.

After a little while, Kusuma came out alone. I carried her in my arms and came away home. "Why did Raji do that when she saw me? Am I a tiger to run away the moment she hears my voice?" I was a little sad. The next time I see her, I will ask her, "Why do you do that when you see me?"

But when will I see her next? Even if I see her, how to talk to her? She runs away the moment she sees me. How to talk to someone like her? No, she is shy. That is why she does this. What is there to ask her? Even if I do ask her, she will be too shy to answer. I have so much money; I am only thirty-five years old. My astrological chart says I will live to be eighty. For a poor girl, isn't it a blessing to find someone like me? She is surely happy that she is getting a wealthy husband. She does all this because of that damned shyness. Poor thing, isn't she still a young girl? After getting married, she won't do all this. Why should I feel bad about a girl's shyness? What will I ask her? Isn't it because her mother knows she will be happy that she agreed to give Raji to me? There is no greater family than a mother. When the mother has agreed, why will the daughter not want this? She is only shy, that's all. Thus, I consoled my saddened heart.

6.

There was still one month left for the day Raji would become my wife. In the last two months I had not seen her even once. Kusuma, as usual, kept going there. She had started staying there all day. Kusuma greatly loved Raji. Sometimes, in her sleep too she would mutter, "Rajakka."

After lunch, I stood outside. Being a Sunday, Raji did not have school that day. I was looking in the direction of Raji's house thinking I'd get to see her if she happened to come out, when the front door of her house opened. Thinking it might be Raji, I waited with great anticipation. The girl who came out was not Raji, but Kusuma. In her hand was a small piece of paper. Seeing me, she came running. When Raji was home, Kusuma wouldn't come back to our house at all. So I was surprised to see her now. She came close and gave me the piece of paper. Before I could ask her who gave it, she had run back to Raji's house. What was this? Wondering why Kusuma had given me the note, I opened it. I saw round letters on the page. I looked to the bottom thinking the writer's name might be written there. There was no name. "Will you please come to the riverbank at five in the evening?" was all that was written.

Who wrote it? What did this mean? Could Raji have written it? Could she who runs away when she sees me have written to me? If not her, who would write this? Kusuma was not there to ask. Whomever it might be, what did I have to lose if I went walking to the river in the evening? I decided that I would go. My heart kept saying that Raji must have written it. I was very happy that at least that day I would see her.

7.

I was ready by four o'clock. In my eagerness to meet Raji, I hurried to the riverbank. The sun was still high so there was no one near the river. Taking great care not to ruin my new suit, I sat carefully on a stone under a tree, waiting for Raji. My heart was dancing with happiness that I would see her in a short while. But the very next instant, my enthusiasm was deflated by a doubt whether the note was written by Raji after all. If she did not come, all the trouble I had taken to get ready would be wasted. Tying and adjusting a tie for an hour before the mirror would be useless! I began to have such thoughts.

If Raji had planned this, why did she ask me to come? Maybe she wanted to say sorry for behaving this way with me. When she started begging saying, "Forgive me for the way I have been acting," how should I talk to her? What all should I tell her? I began to plan. I had been there about half an hour. There was no sign of Raji. What? Did Raji write like that to make fun of me? If not, why had she still not come? When I was thinking all this, I saw Raji in the distance. I was elated that I could now see Raji. My heart was full with happiness. Raji saw me sitting there. But she did not come near me. She went to where several trees were growing close together and there were no people. I followed her there too. Raji was standing under a tree. Since I had just come from the glare of the sun, I couldn't see her face clearly in the shade. Once my eyes adjusted to the shade, I saw Raji's face. The thought that she who was standing like a forest goddess among the trees would soon be the goddess of my home made my heart dance. I did not know what to say. I just stood there looking at her.

8.

Raji did not speak either. She just stood there leaning against the tree. At last, I asked, "Why did you ask me to come, Raji?" She did not speak. I asked again, "Why hesitate with me? Tell me."

After a while she said, "I know you wish to marry me. Please don't. This marriage won't bring either of us happiness. I inconvenienced you so much to tell you this, forgive me."

Raji stood there like a stone. I could not believe my own ears. I thought I had not understood what she had said. Just then, Raji again asked, "Will you kindly fulfil my request?"

This time my illusion vanished. "Raji, what is your problem with this marriage? Your feelings are wrong. If I did not have true love for you, I wouldn't desire to marry you. It is because I know that there is happiness in marrying you that I wish to marry you. You are still a young girl. You don't know anything. If you get married to me, you will not be short of happiness. I can give you whatever jewellery and other things you want. You will be the mistress of my entire wealth. I will always love you. By becoming my wife, your poverty and all other problems will go away…"

Before I could finish my words, Raji asked, "Should I get married to you or your wealth?"

"Raji, if you get married to me, you will be the owner of my wealth. You will be the queen of my love," I said.

She asked, "Did you love your first wife?"

I said, "Yes, but why bring her up now? Now I love you. Be my wife!"

"Now you love me? Who will you love tomorrow? Loved her, it seems! It hasn't even been six months since she died and you are already in a hurry for a second marriage. This is real love now, isn't it?" she said.

Hearing such words come out of Raji's mouth made me a little angry. So much arrogance in a girl from a poor family, I thought and said, "Raji, you are talking like this after reading some novel. You do not know what love is. I love you more than anything else. I can do anything for you. When I love you this much, why are you saying you will not marry me? You might not like that this is a second marriage. But I am only thirty-five years old. I have a lot of property, wealth. When I have all this, what constraint do you have in getting married?" I asked.

9.

Raji kept quiet for a little while and then said, "You are the one who is talking like you have read some novel. I love you more than anything else, you said. I will do anything for you, you keep saying. What you are saying are lies. For me, you will not be able to break your society's rules. You are saying that you are only thirty-five years old. I am fifteen years old. I could be your daughter. You say that I don't know what love is. It is because I know that I do not wish to be your wife. It is because I don't have love for you. You also don't love me. What you have is lust for me. If you really loved your wife, you would not have forgotten her within six months of her death. You would not have neglected her child Kusuma. If you had died and she was alive, would she have married a second time?"

Listening to Raji made me bristle with anger. "Raji….I did not come here to listen to this lecture. Will you marry me or not? Tell me!" I asked.

Raji lifted her face up. Her big, big eyes began to emit fire. Her voice shaking, she said, "Whether I will marry you or not, leave that aside. If you have the guts, if you have the strength to do anything for me like you said, if you truly love me, marry me. I am a child widow."

10.

Raji's words made me feel like I had been hit by thunder. What? The one who I had desired to make my faithful wife, she is a widow? Had I desired to make a widow my equal in marriage, my partner in happiness and despair, the mistress of my incomparable wealth, the queen of my love? I thanked god in my heart for preventing me from unknowingly marrying a widow and bringing disgrace to my lineage. I cursed her mother who wanted to marry off her widowed daughter to me.

Seeing me silent, Raji asked, "What is it? You who said you will do anything for me, will you marry me now?"

I did not have any love now for the Raji whom I had thought I loved. Can a widow be loved? I began to feel great contempt for her. Thinking of how this was the widow I had begged to marry me, I cursed myself. In anger, I answered Raji, "If I knew you were a widow, I wouldn't even have looked at your face. Seeing a widow's face in the morning is inauspicious, and I am not one to marry such a widow."

"Seeing the face of a widow in the morning is inauspicious, fine; but that of a widower? A child does not know what a marriage is, what life's sorrows and joys are, what a husband is. That child is tied around the neck of an old man who dies before she grows out of childhood. She has to spend her entire life being an inauspicious person. But a husband who had children and lived with his wife, can marry an innocent girl and subject her to lifelong punishment the very day after his wife dies, that is fair now, isn't it?" she said.

Trying to cheat me into marrying her apart, that she was saying these things was like adding fuel to fire and my anger increased.

"Should I become the subject of others' mockery by doing things which do not happen in society? Even if it happens in society, I am not ready to spoil my pure family lineage by marrying a widow. I do not have the desire to see a widow's face every morning," I replied.

11.

By the time I was done speaking, Raji was looking at me like a snake which had been stepped on. The one who had looked like a forest goddess to me now seemed like a witch. Her voice shaking with anger, she began to speak. "What did you say? You do not wish to see a widow's face in the mornings? I also don't... I also don't have the desire to see the face of a man who has forgotten his child and wishes to marry again before even six months have passed since his wife's death. You thought I would marry you if you begged me? If I had such a wish, I would not have told you the truth. I am not mad to think the lust perverts like you have is love and marry you. While I am breathing, I will work for the welfare of sisters like me who are burning in the fires of injustice in society. I do not wish to be the mistress of your dirty wealth after accepting the lust of womanizers like you. Lakhs of my sisters are sacrificed to men like you and widowed when we are still children and are subjected to injustice in society. Till this keeps happening, know that Hindu society cannot flourish. How many Hindu widows have taken recourse to a life of impudence because of such social injustice! How many have become prostitutes! So many infanticides and female foeticides are taking place. Do you know? Who is responsible for all this? Is it an innocent little girl? Is it parents who chant the names of scriptures, and fearing that they will lose caste status, marry babies off to old men? Or is it lecherous men like you? No; the fault is not yours; helpless little girls are at fault.

"For someone who keeps taking refuge in scripture, do you even know the smell of it? If you knew, you wouldn't condemn widows like this. Open scriptures like Manusmriti, Vashistasmriti and see. Do you think scriptures go against justice? Yes, it is true that religionists use scriptures to support their arguments. But if they read the scriptures without bias, they would know that the scriptures support widow remarriage. Manu also gave his full support to widow remarriage. You are the one applying a blot to Aryadharma, a religious practice that preaches love. The blot has to be borne by innocent widows. Inhuman cruelty is experienced by widows. The moment the husband dies, the wife's head has to be shaved. If not, they are going against morality, it seems. Even if widowers are old men, they can marry again. Even if it is a child widow, remarriage is forbidden to her. Do you know what impediments have affected Aryadharma as a result of the cruel atrocities meted out to poor widows in the name of morality? Do you know this is the main reason for the decline of Hindu society? Have you ever thought how many widows have converted to other religions because of this cruel treatment? No; it is not right for you to think of all these and spoil your holy lineage. Isn't it? Poor fellow! Without knowing, every day you sat on top of the guava tree and looked at a widow's face. I don't know what all problems you must have faced seeing this inauspicious face. Forget what has happened. From now on at least don't look at the unlucky faces of widows and face problems, understood?"

12.

Raji's words burnt my heart like fire. Every line she spoke stabbed me. Her harsh mockery pierced my heart. The heartache of that child widow came out in her words and gave me a new life. They burnt away my lust. They opened my eyes. My lust for her was destroyed and a kind of devotion took its place. With reverence, I fell at her feet and said, "Devi, I do not have anything to give you in return for your invaluable advice. I swear on your holy feet that I will dedicate this insignificant life of mine to work for the welfare of widows. I pledge my body, mind and wealth at your holy feet for the rights and welfare of widows."

It seems that Raji was surprised seeing my behaviour. Seeing me fall at her feet, "Brother, why are you holding my feet? It is not honourable to fall at the feet of an ordinary widow. But if the pledge you made is true, your mother is really blessed. The purpose of you being born as her son is fulfilled," she said.

Manu's Rani

It was only two months ago that I was transferred to that town. That day, I had had a lot of work. I had left home at six in the morning and only just returned. As I climbed the steps of the house, the hospital clock struck eleven. The children and the servants had all gone to sleep. Only Parvathi was sitting and waiting up for me. I went in, changed my clothes, washed up and was just about to sit down for dinner when we heard someone knock on the front door. Parvathi got irritated: "Thoo, what is this! You left at dawn and came back only now. Someone has already come before you get a chance to eat at least a bit of dinner. Let them keep knocking; I am not going to open the door," she said.

Yes, I was hungry. But…but my heart did not listen. "It's okay, Parvathi. Open the door and see who it is," I said.

She got angrier; "I beg you; you haven't eaten anything since this morning. First, have your food; we will see later," she said.

In the middle of this, the knocking on the door became louder and more urgent. When a human being was struggling between life and death, can I sit and eat? I got up and went to open the door myself. Parvathi's eyes filled with tears. "Our town was better than this damned place where there is no time to even eat," she thought to herself. Though I was hurt to see Parvathi's tear-filled eyes, I couldn't console her just then. I opened the door.

The one who was knocking was a young boy, Subba, the town's good-for-nothing. "What is it?" I asked.

"A big illness in Rajamma's house, it seems. You have to come right away, she said," he replied.

Rajamma! The moment I heard her name, all the sympathy and pity I had felt when I opened the door vanished. "I will come in the morning, go," I said.

He went away. I closed the door and went in. Parvathi felt a little better that I had not gone away like she'd thought I might. Serving me dinner, she asked, "Who was it who came?"

"Subba. To call me to go to Rajamma's house immediately," I said.

Hearing Rajamma's name, "What is wrong with her now! Isn't it enough if you go in the morning? Even if she dies, it is one less burden on earth," she said.

Rajamma, who was scorned even at every utterance of her name, that Rajamma was a prostitute. Though I had never seen her in person, after hearing all that people used to say about her, I thought that she really must be an ogress. "Who will go to her house at this time? I haven't eaten since morning; I can go tomorrow morning," I said to myself and went to bed.

Just then, we heard the sound of someone knocking on the door loudly again. I went and opened the door. Subba! "You have to come right away it seems, doctor. It is serious, it seems. She said to fall at your feet and bring you," he said.

"Who is ill?" I asked.

He did not know. But at least I got to know that it was not Rajamma who was ill. Who else might it be? Whoever it was, even if was Rajamma, it was my duty to go and see. Just because she was a prostitute, what authority did I have to disregard an emergency? Just a while ago, I had kept my duty aside giving myself the excuse that she was a prostitute. I felt ashamed of myself thinking about it. "I will come, wait," I said and went in to quickly get dressed. Parvathi had fallen asleep. I took the medicine bag and left, closing the door behind me.

Rajamma's house was some three-quarters of a mile away from ours; it stood alone inside a plantation. Apart from one or two huts of some poor coolies some ten–twelve yards away, there were no other houses around. When we reached, the door to Rajamma's house lay open. Subbu called, "Ammaaaaa."

Rajamma came out. That was the first time I saw Rajamma. After listening to everything that people had said about her, I had begun to feel that Rajamma was an ogress. But seeing her face shrunk with grief and her eyes red and puffy from crying, I began to feel a lot of sympathy. "Who is not well?" I asked.

Rajamma took me inside instead of answering. There, in a room, a man was sleeping on a cot. Rajamma pointed toward him. I went closer and looked at him. His face was like that of a corpse. Though his eyes were open, it did not look like they had any light of life. I bent down, held his hand and examined him. His hand was burning like fire. He had lost consciousness because of the fever. The minute I examined him, I realized that he was not going to live. Rajamma had placed her head by his feet and was looking in my direction blankly. I have seen several people die. I have heard innumerable people beat their chests and weep uncontrollably. But none of that brought me as much distress as Rajamma's mute lament.

I had seen Rajamma for the first time a little while ago. I had had contempt for her; I had even thought that if she was dying, let her die. But once I saw her crying face, I cannot say why all the prior thoughts I had had about her vanished and were replaced with immense sympathy. It did not look like she was very old. Maybe she was a year or two older than my daughter Shanthi. This kind of plight at such a young age! The reputation of being a famous prostitute!

The sleeping man began to roll about. Though it was impossible to keep him alive with the medicine I had given him, there was a possibility that he might gain consciousness. Rajamma got up from near his feet and began to wipe the sweat on his face. His lips began to shiver. I told her to give him a little water to drink. When she fed him one or two spoons of water, very softly he said, "Rani."

Glancing at me with gratitude, Rajamma said, "What is it, Manu?"

Poor thing, she did not know that the lamp burns brightest just before being extinguished. He cried, "Rani, Rani, Rani," and held her hands.

"I am right here, what is it, Manu?" Rajamma asked.

Again, he loudly screamed "Rani." That was it, that was the end.

It was ten in the morning when I went back home the next day. Both the children had gone to school. The moment I reached, Parvathi rained questions on me, asking "Where did you go? Did you go at night itself, or was it morning? Who was sick?" etc.

But my mind was not in a state to answer her questions just then. It felt like everything from the previous night, the sick man, Rajamma with her dishevelled hair, puffy eyes and wilted face, her mute grief, was still right before my eyes. Though it was Parvathi who was standing before me, to my eyes it looked like Rajamma's shrunken face.

Parvathi must have been surprised to see me standing there, stunned and mute. She felt very sorry thinking that it was because of how much work I had had the previous day. "You didn't sleep all of yesterday; you didn't eat at the right time either. At least now have some tiffin and take rest," she said and brought coffee and breakfast, forcing them on me.

"I don't want anything now, Parvathi. If I sleep and rest for some time, I will be fine," I said and went to bed without even changing my clothes. Thinking that I wanted to sleep, Parvathi started to leave. "Come and sit here, Parvathi," I said. Parvathi came and sat near me. Her questioning look seemed to be asking, "What has happened to you today?"

I told her about all that happened at Rajamma's house the previous night. After listening to the whole account, Parvathi asked, "Who was it who died? What was his relationship with Rajamma?" I had not thought of that until then. Who was it who died? What was the relationship between her and him to cause Rajamma that much grief? I began to wonder too.

Parvathi was very suspicious of Rajamma; "Could Rajamma have poisoned and killed him?" she wondered.

Just a day ago, I would have had the same suspicions as Parvathi. But after seeing Rajamma just once, all such feelings I had had changed. I felt angry at what Parvathi had said. "Be quiet, Parvathi," I said.

My tone must have been harsh; Parvathi's eyes filled with tears in anger. Seeing her face, I felt ashamed of my harshness. Consoling her, I said, "It does not look like Rajamma is the kind of ogress who will poison and kill someone, Parvathi. She must only be a year or two older than our Shanthi. Poor thing, it was very sad to see her. As for people, they will say anything."

It did not look like Parvathi's suspicions of Rajamma had completely gone away. "The man who died must have been rich, she must have killed him for money. Now she is pretending to be grieving to get away with it," was what Parvathi thought.

I did not go to the hospital that day. I kept turning about on the bed under the pretext of taking rest. No matter how much I tried, I couldn't fall asleep though. In the end, I thought I would go for a walk and went out. Without me realizing, my feet took me towards Rajamma's house. The door was open. I went in. Rajamma was sitting on the floor next to the bed the man had been lying on the previous day, and was staring blankly towards the door. Though I had passed through the door and gone in, it did not look like she had seen me. The state she was in was agonizing to see. The corpse had been cremated and she was alone in that house now. Who will go with the prostitute? I felt that I should have brought Parvathi with me. The previous day if anyone had told me to go to Rajamma's house with my wife, I would have certainly fought with them. After seeing her, somehow all such feelings had vanished. When I remembered all the things that I used to think about her, I felt disdain for myself.

She did not realize I was there. "Rajamma," I said.

She quickly turned to me like she would if she was looking at something else. Initially, it did not look like she recognized who I was. I tried a lot to console her. Though she was not crying, it did not seem like my words were consoling her. It was becoming dark. She was alone in that house. But there was nothing I could do. Finally, I said I would send someone for company and left. It was easier said than done, trying to find someone to send to Rajamma's house. In the end, I convinced our house maid to go there for that one night. Shanthi said she would also go with her. Though I did not have a problem with that, Parvathi did not agree to send her.

Since I had not slept for two days, I fell into a deep sleep that night. Parvathi did not wake me up in the morning. So, by the time I woke up, it was past eight. I got ready quickly thinking I would be late for the hospital. When I was walking out of the gate, the maid who had gone to Rajamma's house approached me. In my hurry to get ready, I had forgotten about Rajamma but seeing our maid, I asked how she was doing. She said Rajamma was still sleeping when she left and went in to do her chores.

That day I had a lot of work. By the time I came home for lunch, it was three. After lunch, when Parvathi and I were sitting and talking, she gave me a letter that had come in the afternoon post. I opened the letter. I did not recognize the handwriting. Curious about whose letter it was, I looked for a signature. Rajamma! I was very surprised. What did Rajamma have to write to me about! I began to quickly read:

Doctor,

It is rare for people to have sympathy for people like me. When people like me have a problem, most people think that it is against humanity to help us. All these days—for the past four years I have stopped expecting any help or sympathy from anyone. The other day, all of a sudden, Manu got a high fever.

Except for Subbu, no one else ventures near my house. I sent him to call the doctor. You were not at home. I sent him to ___'s house. He unapologetically said he would not come. Again, I asked him to call you. You said you would come in the morning. Amidst all this, Manu was getting worse every passing minute. I again sent Subbu and asked him to fall at your feet and beg you to come. You had mercy, you came. But I did not have the fortune to keep Manu alive. He is gone.

Who am I and who is Manu? What was our relationship? You must have wondered. You must have also heard what people say about me. Yes. My mother was a prostitute. I was also being groomed to join that profession. My mother wanted to earn a lot of money from me. Her desire was not going to be futile either. A lot of prominent and rich men had liked me and lost their hearts to me. But because of Manu, all my mother's dreams had to remain unfulfilled. Manu—Mohan was his name—was the only son of wealthy parents. Since he had lost his parents when he was a young boy, there was no one to look into his affairs. One day, an old lover of my mother's brought him along to our house. From that day onwards, Manu came to our house all the time, for me. Though my mother had taught me that prostitutes shouldn't have a heart, I had begun to fall in love with Manu. He was also in love with me. My mother did not approve of my relationship with Manu. By then, all of Manu's wealth had fallen into our money chest. That was why he was of no use anymore to my mother.

All of a sudden, Manu stopped coming to our house. When I asked my mother, she said he had gotten married. News of his wedding made me very sad. I took very seriously ill for one or two months. Why didn't I die then! Once I recovered from the fever, I got to know from our maid that Manu had not gotten married, that my mother had told him I had died and that news had made him half mad. I left home that very night. I went to Manu's house. He had gone mad. In his insanity, he had put something in his eyes and become blind. The money he had left after what he had given us had also been spent. But I had with me some jewellery that Manu had given me in his better days. I sold them and got Manu treated. Though his madness *did not get cured completely, he would be alright on some days. But he would get a fever every now and then. My mother had killed the old Manu. My mother had thought that I wouldn't stay with Manu in the state he was in. But she got very angry when she called me and I did not go back with her. It became difficult for me to stay there after that. In the end, Manu and I left that town and came here. As the days passed, Manu completely lost his mind. No matter what we tried, he could not be cured. Except for calling me "Rani", he would not talk much either. But he would know when I came close to him. If I went away, he would call, "Rani." We were in this house for three years. He is not here now. What work do I have here now?*

Doctor, why am I writing all this to you? In all these years, you and Subbu are the only two people who have behaved with humanity and sympathy with us. That is why I had to write this to tell you before I leave. I can never forget your help in Manu's last moments. What can a wretched animal like me give you in return? Only god has to keep you well.

Rajamma

After reading the letter, I gave it to Parvathi. She also read the letter. Her eyes filled with tears. "What a sinner I am," she said.

My heart was feeling strange. It too said, "what a sinner I am", as if echoing Parvathi's words.

That evening, when I was about to go for a walk, Parvathi said she would come too. Both of us went to Rajamma's house. But she had left before we got there.

Who knows where she had gone!

False Dream

26.5.28

Passing the time is such a heavy burden. I cannot write how difficult it is to bear. There is no one to talk to. There are no books that I want to read. Even if there were, how will I read? When I came from his house, I forgot my book there. I forgot the book, leave that, but there is something bigger that I couldn't bring with me.

Shantha's letter has come. It is a pleasant letter, just like I expected it to be.. But can it soothe my burning heart? Can it bring happiness to my heart? Whom shall I tell…these are not words I can share…what shall I do…?

God should not have given memories to humans. How cruel! What stubbornness! All my attempts to escape were in vain. There is no way I can escape from the web of memories I am trapped in. Nature has built a beautiful abode around my house. Will the cruelty of memories spare me if I go to see its glorious beauty? No, it is impossible. What else shall I turn to? A book? That's also over. How can a dry book be equal to a budding memory? Mother, father and Lalitha will go to the village the day after tomorrow. I'll be alone in the house. A feast of memories will eat me up. Is this the rule of the universe? Hardship…wherever I see, hardship. No one is happy. Don't I too need some sort of hardship? Yes! Then why should I be sad? What is the use of telling anyone? It feels like it is better to be quiet. But how will I be quiet?

3.6.28

The whole family has gone to the village. Only Akka and I are at home. She has household chores; once that is over, then Ramayana. For me, always a festival of memories…the more I think of forgetting, the more I remember. Just yesterday his letter came. What harsh words….poor thing! How will he ever know the fire burning in the depths of my heart? Even if his letter was harsh, I found sweetness in it too. Even if lips are crooked, tender kisses— is the pleasure of those kisses crooked? When I love him, can his rude letter be short of sweetness for me?

He writes to me once a week. Even if his letters came every day, every minute, I would still not be satisfied. Then how will the heat in my heart be satiated by the four lines he writes once a week? What are you thinking, Akka asks. What will I reply to her? Shall I lie? It is not my habit to tell lies. But now how can I not? Akka loves me a lot. If I am a little sad, she feels immensely sad. I am ashamed of deceiving an elder sister who loves me so much. What shall I do?

Kripa will come at four o'clock, it seems. If she comes, I can ask her about him. But how will I ask her? If I ask her, what if she guesses what is in my heart? No, Kripa is not the kind to give space to such thoughts, somehow I will ask her. How can I not ask her? Aiyo! Can't four o'clock come fast? Why is every minute as long as an eon…?

4.6.28

Kripa came. I asked her too. All of last night, the same news….Kripa is bored of telling me the same thing. For me…but for me…I am not satisfied no matter how many times I hear it. Shall I ask once more? If I ask, what will she think? Let her think whatever she wants, I'll ask her…no…I can't ask…burning heart, bear a little…Kripa is calling… why might she be calling? I have a letter, it seems. Whose might it be? Could it be his? What if it is not? What a blow to my hopes it will be! Yes, it is his…what has he written? He will come, he says…he will come tomorrow…dear heart, do not burst with happiness…tomorrow! When will it be tomorrow? Why isn't this day getting over quickly? Why isn't even sleep showing me mercy?

6.6.28

How quickly two days go by! Time that was heavy, time that could not be borne, how fast that time flew when he was here! Couldn't those two days never get over…those happiness-filled days, will they ever come again? What if they don't come? Those reminiscences, those sweet memories will always stay alive in my heart….

The feelings I have in my heart when I think of yesterday…I cannot write those…how can I ever write them? Can I ever do justice by writing them down? If I write, they will only become more intense, oh god! Will those days come back ever again?

I had risen from bed before it even struck five o'clock that morning; it was barely even dawn yet. After washing my face, I filled my hands with jasmine flowers from the plant I had lovingly planted and nurtured. When I was coming in, there he was. He had woken up and was coming to wash his face. When I saw him, I cannot describe all that happened in my heart. The more I try to explain, the harder it seems. Words cannot contain the feelings I had in that moment. Every time I see him, I feel like that. No matter how hard I try to hide my feelings, my eyes bring them out from the deepest parts of my heart. He saw me and asked, "Why did you wake up before dawn?"

No words came out of my mouth. I flung the jasmine buds I had just plucked at his face and ran away. I don't know what he thought of my strange behaviour.

In the evening we all went out for a walk. I have never seen nature flaunt her beauty the way she was that day. Maybe it was because he was with me that nature looked so fetching to my eyes. I will never be able to say this again…but that evening will never ever fade from my heart. Kripa and my sister were walking a little ahead of us. The two of us were walking together, a little behind them. I do not know what Kripa and my sister were talking about—though I could hear them, my mind was elsewhere and there was no chance I could understand their words. While walking, he suddenly stopped. I also stopped with him. Kripa and my sister did not notice us stopping and kept walking. They continued talking and walked even further ahead. I do not know how long we stood there like that. In the end, he broke the silence and asked, "Sarasa, why did you do that in the morning?"

I did not speak.

"Sarasi, why aren't you talking? I do not know why you did that. But the effect it had on me….Sarasa…my Sarasa….," he said.

No more words left his mouth. He held me against himself and rained kisses on me. How much time was spent like that, I cannot say. Upon hearing my sister calling from a distance, he let my hand go—unable to stand, I sat down.

In a loving tone, he said, "My Sarasa, forgive me; I will never do this again. Forgive me this one time."

Before I could reply, my sister came. Without talking much, we came back home.

After dinner that night, eating from the betel nut tray she brought out, Kripa asked, "Why aren't you taking any, Sarasi?"

I took two betel leaves, applied lime paste on them and put one in my mouth. By then, he also joined us. When Kripa went to keep the tray inside, I placed the leaf I had prepared in his hand. He held both my hands and asked, "Is this a sign of forgiveness?"

"Forgiveness is only for those who have committed a crime, isn't it?" I asked.

Listening to my words he said, "Sarasa, may god protect you, that is my only prayer," he pressed my hands to his eyes and left.

The next morning when I went to wash my face, he was standing near the jasmine plant. Seeing me, he asked, "Shall I pluck the flowers for you, Sarasa?"

While I was washing my face, he plucked the flowers and put them in a bowl fashioned from a leaf. Once I had washed my face, he pressed it into my hands…I did not know what to say…I looked at his face…looking intensely at me, he said, "Sarasi, I will leave at ten o'clock. How can I stay without you, tell me? Will you write to me?"

I could not speak. My eyes welled up and I could not see through my tears.

He wiped my tears with his handkerchief, "Don't cry, Sarasa, if you cry, I will feel very sad. Every tear of yours will prick my heart. Tell me you will write to me with a smile," he said.

What I replied, I don't remember now. Whatever it was, whatever I said, what does it matter? He loves me. What more do I need?

8.10.30

Marriage! So many people are elated by the mention of marriage; marriage is the highway to happiness, they say. Is that true?

It might be true for brides who get to marry those they love. For me? But for me? Why does marriage seem worse than dying? Whom shall I ask? Even if I ask, who will give me an answer? Shall I beg god? I would beg if there was a god. If he was there….aiyo, why should I blame god? Why doesn't father have mercy? Who shall I appeal to? Mother is not on this earth. Akka? But who will listen to Akka? How can I be the bride in a wedding where he is not the groom? What will he think? Shall I open his letter that came yesterday? Why don't I have the courage? Let it be, I will read it…. aiyo….what has he written? His prayer to god is that my future life be full of joy and happiness, he writes. Joy! Happiness! How funny…happiness when he is not there? He also cannot understand me, is it? How can I forget him? That evening…that evening when we went for a walk…is it possible for me to forget it? His loving face when he gave me a handful of jasmine flowers and said, "keep writing letters to me," eyes that were radiating love, how can I push out all those feelings from my heart? Aiyo…his letters…the love that emanated from every word….who knew this would happen? Why can't I go mad?

6.4.31

Blows from a stick can be borne; it is hard to bear kicks from the pen. That too when I read the words from his pen, even my stone-like heart is melting. Why does the will to keep the strict vow I made to myself on the day of the wedding leave me when I read his letters? "How cruel you are, Sarasi, why are you not replying to any of my letters?" he has written. Yes, I am cruel…because of the cruelty father subjected me to, I am now a cruel person to him…this is today's justice. What shall I do? What shall I write? Shall I refrain from writing? What will he think? Was I born to suffer this kind of anguish? Why can't I die? Shall I jump into the well? I cannot…I have a sister who loves me more than her life. I have a husband who considers me more important than his life. What do I have to give in return for the kind of love they give me? Whatever I had, I offered it to him a long time ago…what is left now? With devotion I do small and big things for my husband with much care. But that which is important is not with me. What to do? I cannot die…I cannot live… what shall I do? What shall I do? Whom shall I ask for help?

18.10.31

Tomorrow is his wedding, it seems! Let it be…what is it to me? Why should I say aiyo? For three years when I have been praying, "let him get married soon, let him forget me," why should I hear of his wedding today and feel sad? Why should he stay unmarried for my sake? I have given my heart so many excuses, but still deep within, why is it saying "aiyo" in a small voice? Let it be…let him get married… may god protect them both…may his family life be a happy one….

21.3.34

He is coming tomorrow with his wife and child. Oh god, when he is here, have mercy on me and ensure that I don't express my nervousness before his wife. Oh heart, be quiet…let me bear this flutter. What shall I talk to him? How will I show this face to him?

Oh god, prevent my eyes from showing the secret of my heart before him tomorrow....

22.3.34

He has come and sat down with his wife and child. How will I show him my face? What shall I say? How will I go outside? It won't do to not go meet them. What is he saying? "Are you well, Sarasi?" Yes, I am well. I am very happy that you came with your wife and child. What is your child's name? Prabha? That is a nice name...I like that name... come here, Prabha...how adorable is the child? The moment I called she smiled and came to me. She is looking at me with eyes that are just like his. The same wide eyes as his, the same nose, the same red lips, is he looking through the pure eyes of the child? His wife, she is a suitable partner for him...her smiling face...yes, she is a suitable wife for him. There is joy and happiness evident on his face. He is now happy. May god always keep him like this...may god protect his wife and child...that is my prayer....

Me! Why should I desire happiness in a world of sorrow? I do not have any right to be happy...but god! Just do not give me memories. Detach me from the web that memory has spun around me. Save me from the clutches of memories that sprout anew the more I try to forget...why am I not going mad?

Four Incidents

1.

Seetha,

"Write soon; I will be waiting, don't forget," you have written. Forgive me for not writing. It is not because I have forgotten you like you thought, and it is not because I have new friends. Can there be any friend more important than you? What reason shall I give? I will not try. Excuses are not necessary when you trust me. You know me, so why explain further?

My Seetha, even if I write you a letter every second, it still won't be enough for me. For the number of letters that I write to you, even if the government establishes a post office next to my house, they won't suffer any loss.

I was happy to know that you passed in your exam. In my previous letter, "don't pass", I had written. You must have guessed that it was because of my selfishness that I wrote that. You having passed is a matter of great joy and pride. I have also started learning the Hindi language. Do I have to say it is because of you? I think of John Ruskin's "Of Queen's Gardens". They say that if men have the support of women, they can accomplish anything. If the men of the Hindu country had someone like my Seetha, by now the whole country would have been one in language.

Seetha, you have already given me a lot of nicknames. This time, you will not be able to resist calling me chatterbox, I know. In this age when titles are fought over, this is not fair, is it? But when you give me honorifics which, even after much difficulty, are not possible to acquire, is it wrong to say that I am lucky?

But you have to come and give me the title in person. Do not just send a letter, okay?

Yours,
Ramu

2.

Seetha,

Why are you angry? Have you decided not to write at all? But I know, Seetha, how soft your heart is; when you see this letter, you will forget your anger and start writing to me, I know. The heart of beautiful Hindu women is very soft—that too my Seetha's heart!

The other day when I was returning from the club, there was an incident that made me understand that trying to discover the depths of a woman's tolerance, love, devotion and trust is not easy.

You know the road I take to go to office every day. You have seen our office peon Thimma's house by the side of the road. Thimma, his wife, and their one-year-old child are the only people in that house. Thimma's child is always playing by the door to the street. If you apply ash on the body of that child, the ash itself might look white, that is how dark that child is. But still the child is very cute. Isn't the charm of its face enough?

The other day, I was returning from the club by the same road. It was past eight o'clock. All the doors of houses were shut. The light from a lamp was peeping into the street from inside Thimma's house. I could hear loud cries from within. When I went closer, I got to know that Thimma was beating his wife. By the time I walked a few steps past the house, Thimma had dragged her out to the road and was beating her hard with a stick. People from neighbouring houses began to open their doors to come out and see. Seeing this, I thought, "this too is family life."

The next morning, I was going to office by the same route. Thimma was repairing the broken fence in front of his house. His wife was standing close by and was laughing and talking to him. Like every other day, their child was playing in the yard. Just as I was going past, she lifted the child up and placed it on Thimma's shoulders. The child clapped its hands and started laughing. She also laughed. Thimma smiled and began to kiss his child. To say that I was shocked to see this is not surprising, is it Seetha? If this were a Western country, a new application for divorce would have been filed already.

Yours,
Ramu

3.

Seetha, when I said that they were going to table a bill to ensure that daughters also got a share in their father's property, you laughed and teased me, saying, "You don't have sisters, Ramu, that is why you have such guts." Do you remember? But your heart knows, even if I don't have sisters, I will not be against the financial independence of women. Isn't it? Tell me the truth.

Yesterday, I went to the estate. By the time I returned, it was dark. You know how cold it gets now. I had forgotten to wear a coat. Shivering from the cold, I was thinking, "let me get home soon." I was walking fast. I had reached the big Nandi flame tree on the way to the estate. It looked like someone was sitting under the tree. Didn't Bira say there was a ghost under the Nandi tree? I pointed a torch and looked—not because I believed in ghosts, but to see who was sitting there. It was a woman. A child was sleeping on her lap. Even though the mother was shivering in the cold, the child, in the safety of her saree veil, was sound asleep. Eyes red from crying, hair in disarray, torn saree. Seeing her sitting alone in the dark with a child, I asked her why she was sitting there. Aiyo Seetha, if you had been there with me, you would not have laughed when I brought up the issue of women's financial independence.

That orphan widow's mother-in-law had fought with her and thrown her out of the house with the child in the middle of the night.

What do you say to this, Seetha? If you understand how badly women are being affected by the lack of financial independence by just this one example, I will be really happy.

What else shall I write?

Yours,
Ramu

4.

My Seetha,

Your letter came last week. But I was not in town. I returned just now. There was a stack of letters on the table. I knew that your letter would have come. I quickly opened and read it and read it again; I am not satisfied no matter how many times I read it, Seetha! If I sit and keep reading it, replying to you will be delayed. If I reply slowly, you will also do the same. That is why I will first write you a letter, and until you write in reply, I will keep reading this one. Write soon. Do not try to take revenge thinking I delayed replying this time. If you knew the reason for this delay, you wouldn't do that.

I have written that I was not in town when your letter came. Do you know where I went? To Govinda Rao's house; for his grandson's naming ceremony. I went a day early; they had insisted. It was a child born after a long wait—the doll of everyone in the house. The preparations for the naming ceremony were underway with great gusto.

The daughter-in-law who had gone for the delivery hadn't come back. The son had gone to bring her. It had been a little while since I had arrived. I was sitting on the veranda, chatting with the other guests. By then, their son came with his wife and child. It was ten in the morning. Govinda Rao's wife received them, pampered the child and to ward off any evil eye, placed a dot of soot on his face. She put some kumkum on her daughter-in-law's forehead, held her hand and took her inside.

Everyone was happy, celebrating in high spirits. A child had been born in the house after a long time. That too an adorable ball of a male child. (Don't laugh) Need you ask, the shower of happiness!

The daughter-in-law went inside. The mother-in-law made the daughter-in-law sit on a mat spread out on the jagali (a raised platform in the rear of the house), and brought milk for the grandson. The new mother began to feed him milk. There were just about two spoons of milk left. Just then there was a loud "damm!" sound. The mother who was feeding her son milk fell over. The child fell to the ground and started screaming. We all ran to see what happened. The grandmother lifted the child up while the son lifted up his wife. Blood was flowing from her chest like a flood. Before she was lifted up from the ground, her life had flown away.

Just an instant ago, she was revelling in the pride of motherhood and glowing in the charm of youth. And now she had left the joys and sorrows of this lifetime and gone away. Everybody stood like statues, not knowing what to do. The child alone was screaming and crying. The child's father had lost consciousness.

After a while we got to know: the cause of her untimely death was a bullet fired to scare away crows in the orange orchard in the backyard. It had accidentally hit her.

Look Seetha, the kind of sorrow that fell upon the family that was immersed in peace, joy and happiness at the birth of the grandson! The way it fell upon them!

Not knowing that death might be around the corner, people fight with each other. Is that what life's secret is? Who knows?

Always yours,
Ramu

He Was Gone!

Sometimes, the truth is more surprising than imagination. Sometimes, it is as unnatural as fiction. What I am about to narrate belongs to this category. Those who hear it will surely say that I imagined all of it. That is why I have carefully kept all the newspaper clippings related to this. Whoever has any doubt can come and inspect them. Then really, you will understand that 'truth beats imagination'.

Five of us friends from the same village studied together in college and were returning home during vacations. Apart from us, there was an old man in the compartment we were sitting in. I don't know why that old man felt like telling us this story. We were talking about a murder committed a few days ago. Silent until then, the old man suddenly asked, "Shall I tell you a story?" He looked like a good man. How could we be rude and say, "We don't wish to listen to your story?" Though we were not interested, we signalled our consent.

The old man started his story thus, without much preface:

This is a story from thirty years ago. The person I am talking about was then a healthy young man of twenty-five. He had lost his parents at a very young age and was growing up in someone else's house. They were not family, and it was difficult for them to give him clothes and food to begin with. On top of that, where would the money come from for education! The wife of the man who raised him was a good woman. Thanks to her mercy, he learnt to read and write a little; that was his education. Once he turned eight or ten, he began working for the people in that house. Initially, he used to look after the calves. The older he grew, the more work he began to get. He did not feel bad about working. He used to work from morning till night. Where else would they get such a trustworthy, hardworking servant? That too, without having to pay a salary! He was trusted and liked by the people in the house.

This way, one day after the other, years went by. He also grew older. A strong body that was six feet tall, a serious face filled with health, eyes beaming with energy, all this made him stand out tall even among the hundreds of other workers in the fields that belonged to that household.

Though he worked in the fields, he still lived in their house. He ate the same food that they did. After finishing work in the fields, tying the cattle back in the shed, milking the cows, tying the calves separately and feeding them all hay, by the time he got back home, it would be time to light the lamp. That was also his job. After lighting the lamp, he had to bathe the small children at home; this was the last of his daily duties. By then it would be seven thirty. Once the bathed children sat down to study, he would also go sit in a corner and turn the pages of their books. That was how he had not forgotten the little he had learnt to read and write as a child.

He would get food at nine o'clock. Once he had eaten, he would go to sleep, wake up again at four in the morning and begin working.

His life was programmed like this, with no difference from one day to the next. He did not have time to wonder whether he was satisfied or dissatisfied with his life. Even if he did have time, such thoughts hadn't occurred to him. By the time some changes began to occur in his life without him knowing, he was about twenty-four years old.

That year, they had finished the field work earlier than usual. That was why he got more free time than he'd ever had before. That same year, the family's mestri, the supervisor, died, and he got that job. Now he had to get other people to work, and not work himself. This apart, he began to get a little salary as well, though not as much as the old mestri used to get.

Having never had even a single paise to call his own, he was happy and satisfied with the little he now got.

As I told you before, that year, he had finished the work in the fields early. It is common practice in the village to go to one's neighbours' fields to help out once one's own work is finished. Though he was now a mestri, he did not give up the practice of helping out the neighbours. He would go with four to six workers to others' fields every day.

Even if there is torrential rain, even if the cold is such that it births shivers in the body, there is an enthusiasm in working in the fields with many people. Singing songs, chatting away, one forgets what tiredness is. There is no ennui in working in the fields during the times of planting and harvesting. He was never lazy. Work was for him play; others were also enthused while working with him. Both men and women would work together in the fields, that was the practice. During planting season, the women would remove the saplings and tie them together. The men would do the transplanting. There would be a competition to see who would remove more saplings and who would transplant more. There was no one to beat him in transplanting. That day, the woman who gave him saplings at the speed that he was transplanting them was the one who completely changed his life. She was from the Muslim community.

What does love have to do with caste and community? It is blind. Though if it is true love, its path is not without obstacles.

Having always worked through rain and shine, she was a little dark, but her built was pleasing, along with a full, wide face. Those who saw her enthusiasm for work would say, "It is difficult to find a girl like Latifa in any community." The Muslim girl who stole his heart was Latifa.

That was their very first introduction. It is enough to say this much. It is not necessary to say how their love grew.

He did not have anyone to call his own. She had a mother who was now married to another man. Her mother had children from that marriage too. Latifa's was not a happy life in her stepfather's house. It was not difficult for people working in neighbouring fields to see each other. By the time six–seven months went by, he was ready to give up his religion for her. And she! She was ready to give up her life for him.

But where is the place for a love like that in this world? Her stepfather saw them both talking one day; he became suspicious immediately. He decided right away to get Latifa married off soon. Who wouldn't agree to marry a girl like that? The Muslim man next door, who had children, and who had lost his wife a month ago, was ready. Latifa's stepfather got a hundred rupees from him and agreed to give her to him. There was no question of asking Latifa's opinion for this relationship. She also knew that well. The only thought she had was to go and tell him. But her stepfather had taken care to make sure she did not leave the house.

That day, as usual, he waited for her. Even when the clock struck seven, there was no sign of her. Though he could not be at peace without seeing her, he had no choice but to go his owner's house to light the evening lamp. He sent his heart towards her and went home.

The next day, he woke up an hour earlier than usual. He finished all his morning chores quickly, waited till everyone was drinking coffee and left for her house. She was milking the cow in the shed, and seeing him, left the milk pot there and ran towards him.

When she told him of her sorrows, he stood there, immobile with helplessness. She went on saying, "I cannot live without you; kill me with your own hands," and continued to cry. I cannot say now whether he was in his senses or not then. But it is true that if I had loved her like him and there came a situation where I had to give her up to another man, then I would have also done what he did. He did not have the strength then to think logically. He could have taken her and gone away somewhere. But he was not a man who could think of things like that. He did not want to take her away like a thief without marrying her. His heart too was not in a state to think too much at the time.

I don't know what he thought! She was at his feet, saying "Kill me." He lifted her up, wiped her tear-soaked face, kissed her gently on her wide forehead and said, "Don't cry, Lati, let's go together. You don't have any problem coming with me, do you?"

She held his legs again and said, "Instead of marrying him, it is better that I die at your hands. Kill me."

He lifted her up again, held her face between his hands and saw his reflection in her serious eyes that were filled with peace. "Are you ready?" he asked. The face that half a second ago had been bleak with tears now beamed with a smile. Looking at him steadfastly, her eyes said, "Yes." He could not bear it, the mute permission he read in her eyes; he pulled her close and pressed her face to his chest. In the next second when his grip loosened, she had become a corpse. His knife was in her body, piercing her back into her chest. The smile that had lit her face just an instant ago, the peaceful look in her eyes, remained as they were.

But he could not see any of this. He did not see the body lying in a pool of blood. Standing on the other side of all the binds of caste and religion, she was calling him with a smile on her face, and he jumped into a well nearby to join her.

He jumped into the well to join her in death; but he did not die, he did not die…

The old man told us all this and became quiet for a while. Before he began the story, we had been disinterested but now, we felt like weeping. Wondering what he might think if he saw us weep, we hid our faces and wiped our tears. But the old man was not looking at us. He was staring into space. His eyes were filled with grief. Looking at him, we wondered whether the "he" in the story was a relative of this old man. What happened to "him"? We were all curious, but kept quiet until the old man began talking again.

After some time, the old man said:

Her stepfather, wondering why she hadn't come in yet, came out, saw him jumping into the well and pulled him out. There was a case in the court, but he did not know any of it. People said he had gone mad. He did not get the death sentence because he had gone mad. It would have been good if he had been sentenced to death. He had thought that even if he could not join her by jumping into the well, at least the death sentence would take him near her. Unlucky fellow! He was not even that fortunate!

Though he was not mad, he spent thirty years in a mental hospital as a mad man. Don't ask, "How did he spend those thirty years?" If I tell you how he spent those years, even those who are sane might go mad. Though his life's desire was to go be with her, he could not find a way to do so. And he spent those years amidst mad people, becoming madder than them. After thirty years, he was released one day. "He was released, he can go now," you might say. Yes, he can go now. Yes, I am leaving now…I will go now.

What is this! We all looked at each other's faces, wondering if he had gone mad himself while narrating the story. By the time we looked at him again, fast as light, he had jumped out of the window of the moving train.

Stunned, we pulled the chain and stopped the train.

But this time, he had finally left to be with Latifa who had waited for him for thirty years.

Fate's Game

1.

The day that Mani came, Malathi was playing pagade, a board game played with dice and pawns, with Latha from the house across the road. Around that time, Mani and Raja had finished drinking coffee and gone out for a stroll. Baby Manohar was playing on the veranda with Latha's sister.

Malathi had lost the last two games. Though she was playing very cautiously this time, it did not look like she was going to win. Wanting to stop playing before she lost and Latha made fun of her, she said, "Thoo, I am bored. Leave this," and lifted the board.

Latha who had thought, "I am just about to win" did not like Malathi's behaviour. "Look at you now! You say you are bored when you are about to lose," she said a little harshly and got up.

Malathi was much older than Latha. She had forced the girl to stop reading and come and play with her. She was also worried that the girl would get upset. She held her hand and said, "Let it go, Latha. Why so much anger? You won, I lost. Did your anger go away now?"

Latha laughed and said, "You lost, didn't you? Remember this…"

"Wait till tomorrow, I'll avenge my loss…," Malathi said, and began to fold the mat.

"We'll see who is going to lose," Latha said and turned towards the door, but came back to say, "Hey, someone is standing at the door, I can't go past him."

"Ayyo, mad girl, go away! Can't you tell them to give you way? Come," Malathi said and walked to the front door with Latha.

Mani was standing at the door. "I thought it was someone else. What, Latha, didn't you know Mani has come? Give some space for Latha, Mani," said Malathi. The moment Mani gave way, Latha slid through the door and disappeared.

Watching her leave, Mani asked, "Who is that girl, Akka?"

Malathi replied, "She is Rama Rayaru's daughter from the house across the road."

2.

It was around three in the afternoon, Mani had shut the door to his room and was writing a letter to a friend of his. He must have written some four lines, when Manohar started banging on the door incessantly, saying, "Mani maama, open the door."

Mani answered from his room, "Don't be naughty, dear Manu. If you stay quiet, I'll take you out for a walk in the evening."

Satisfied, Manohar ran away. Not even five minutes after Mani resumed writing his letter, there was another knock on the door. This time, Mani got angry. "Are you making noise again after I told you to be quiet? I won't take you out for a walk, you bad boy," he scolded. But having heard Latha's giggles instead of Manohar crying, Mani abandoned the letter he was writing and opened the door. In these last two months, he had gotten used to seeing, talking to and being friendly with Latha, who came to his Akka's house frequently. That was why he asked a little angrily: "What is this, Latha? One or the other, you all make noise."

Poor Latha was not used to seeing Mani angry. Her eyes filled with tears. "What can I do? Your sister asked me to come and call you. That is why I knocked," she said.

Even if Mani did not notice her tear-filled eyes, Mani realised she was hurt from her tone. He was a little ashamed too of his short temper. Trying to console her, he said, "See Latha, I am writing a letter. Tell her I'll finish writing and come."

After Latha left, Mani sat down again to write. But the very next moment, there was another knock on the door. "Now there is no hope of writing," Mani thought to himself and opened the door. This time it was Malathi who had come. Could Malathi be scolded!

"Come, let's play one game," she insisted and dragged Mani out of his room.

Malathi's husband Raja, and Latha were sitting with the pagade board in front of them, and Malathi said, "Mani and I are one party, you both are one party," and began to play.

Mani had not played pagade in a long time and was out of practice. But Malathi thought that since Raja also was not an expert, somehow, she could defeat Latha easily. Defeating her was not easy. Latha played ferociously, not wanting to lose. In the end, it was Malathi's party that lost. Raja, who had expected to lose, said to Mani upon winning, "What Mani, you are a rank holder in exams and you lost in just one game? Listening to your sister praise you, I thought you'd certainly win."

Latha who was serious until then, began to giggle, as if to tease, "Did you see? Did you see who won?"

Mani retorted, "Let's see, Bhaava, let's play another game. We will definitely win this time," and started putting the pagade board back in order.

Hoping to win by any means and get even, Malathi said, "What is the big deal if you won one game? Let's play three games and whoever wins two, let's consider they won the match, okay?" Latha agreed.

Raja asked, "All that is fine, Malathi. But what prize will the winner get? You did not say that."

"What prize? Isn't winning itself enough?" asked Malathi.

"I don't agree. Who will come to play just like that? My clients must be waiting for me in the office. How can I sit here playing?" asked Raja and began to get up.

What a moment he chose to get up! A client came home looking for him at that very instant. Raja left the game and went away.

Having begun to play with a lot of enthusiasm, Malathi did not want to end the game. Latha also wanted to defeat Malathi once more. Not just her, Latha also wanted to mock Mani who had boasted about winning. Mani was eager to avenge his defeat. But the game needed either another player, or Mani had to leave. What was to be done?

Finally, Malathi declared, "Let me and Latha play first. The winner can play with Mani. Whoever wins that match is the winner."

Mani agreed and moved aside. Latha and Malathi began to play. Mani watched the game very enthusiastically, and realised that Latha was going to win. He was astounded at the way Latha was collecting all the pagade pieces even though his sister was playing so well. What small hands! How beautiful those graceful fingers were, he thought, and his admiration of the beauty of her hands became the reason he suddenly lost interest in playing. He began to note how many bangles Latha wore on her tiny wrists, what kind of bangles they were and so on. It was not that Mani had not looked at Latha earlier. He had seen her, and spoken to her with a sort of negligence, as the little girl from the house across the road who used to come to play with his sister. But now when he began to really look at her, Mani realized she was a beautiful girl.

Mani had guessed correctly; Latha won the game. Maybe it was because Mani was sitting right there, that her laughter did not erupt too much. That was exactly what Malathi wanted too. "I am spared," she thought.

Mani tried controlling his laughter and asked, "How did this happen, Akka?"

Having noticed his feeble attempts to hold his laughter in, Malathi knew that she did not want to see him burst out laughing and quickly said, "I'll go keep water to boil for coffee and come. You both start playing," and quietly escaped.

3.

Mani did not have the heart to play with Latha. He knew he might have to lose to her. Neither could he forfeit. Instead, he said, "I'll play if we play for something, not otherwise."

Knowing it would be easy to win against Mani, Latha did not want to leave; yet she was not for pledging something for the game. "I don't have anything to pledge," she said.

While playing with Malathi, Mani had noticed a ring on her small fingers. "If you lose, you have to give me your ring, if I lose, I'll give you mine," he said.

Latha was extremely confident of winning, so she said, "Hmm, okay."

Left with no excuse, Mani sat down to play.

If Mani had concentrated, maybe he would have won. But since his attention was less on the game and more on Latha's beauty, he ended up losing. Before he could remove his ring and give it to her, Latha giggled and ran away to where Malathi was.

Mani had begun to think Latha was a beautiful girl, Now, after seeing the laughter in her eyes, his opinion on her beauty became stronger. "Latha is like a swaying lathe, a beautiful creeper. Her eyes are like the flowers on the lathe," he thought to himself and continued to sit by the pagade board.

Just then, Malathi came out, teasing him, "So you too lost to Latha!"

At the same time, Latha told Malathi, "I'll come back," and ran away.

Though Latha had run away, her reflection remained in Mani's heart. This was all he thought about that whole night: Latha was not from a well-to-do family. So what if she was not as beautiful as a movie star or not educated enough to talk about international affairs? She knew how to read and write well; she was not short of qualities that would make her a good wife who could keep her husband happy. With a face on which waves of laughter kept swirling the man who married her would be a fortunate one. Could that good luck be mine? But the moment Mani had this thought, he shrunk into himself. What good qualities did he have that Latha would agree to marry him? Why would her father approve someone who could not afford to support a wife? Even if he approved, how could he look after her? Thanks to Raja's generosity, he could study. But what now?

Mani had been looking for work since the day his exams got over. Though he had not been successful until then, he had not worried about it much. But now every time he saw Latha, his only thought was—work work work.

In between all this, Rama Rayaru had started inviting Mani to his house frequently. Mani went thinking he would get to see Latha. Every time he went, it was Latha who would come and serve him tea.

One day, Malathi asked him, "Mani, do you know why Rama Rayaru keeps inviting you to his house?"

He replied, "For tea."

Malathi teased him, "For tea, it seems!"

Mani looked up at her, surprised. Malathi laughed and said, "You don't know anything. Still a child."

Mani was flustered thinking his sister must have gotten to know that he was in love with Latha. Still, he asked her, "What, Akka, what do you mean?"

"You are a smart boy, kano. Acting as if you don't know anything. Anyway, let me only tell you. They want to get Latha married to you. We also approve. What do you say?" she asked.

Though he had spent time building castles in the air, Mani had not thought that a fellow like him would get Latha to be his. He was very surprised that it was her family that was interested in the match. He did not know what to say. Seeing him remain silent, Malathi asked, "You will not find a girl like Latha even if you go searching, Mani. What is wrong with her? Isn't she beautiful?"

Mani asked, "Why marriage for me, Akka? I don't even have a job."

"Fine, just because you don't have a job now, does it mean you will never get one? You are a rank holder. How will you not get a job? Don't give such excuses," Malathi said.

It was true that Mani was in love with Latha, but he did not have the heart to get married before he had work and a house to look after his wife. That was why, when Malathi asked that night, "What Mani, haven't you finished thinking," he replied, "I will marry Latha if she is willing to wait until I get a job. I don't want to get married without a job in hand."

Raja and Malathi both agreed to this. Latha's parents wanted to get her married that very year. But where would they get a good groom like Mani? So they also agreed to wait.

4.

Since it was decided that Latha would marry Mani, she stopped coming to Malathi's house. Even if Mani went to her house, he could not see her. Ever since Mani knew that Latha was the girl he was going to marry, he wanted to talk to her and get to know her. He finally got an opportunity to fulfil this dream.

One evening Mani got ready to go out for a walk. Just then Malathi said, "Don't go anywhere today, Mani. I am bored, let's play at least one game of pagade."

Mani replied, "No, Akka. I am tired of sitting. Play with Latha," and started to leave.

"Latha never comes over. What will I do now?" Malathi laughed.

"She doesn't come because I am here, isn't it? I am leaving now," he replied, and left.

After he left, Malathi went to Latha's house and forced her to come. By then, Mani had returned from his walk. "What is this, Mani, you said you were going to go for a stroll?" Malathi asked.

"I did not find Bhaava to come with me, and I felt bored to go alone. You were calling me to play too, so I came back," Mani replied and sat down on the mat.

Latha, who was chatting away with Malathi until then, became too shy to even raise her eyes.

Malathi said, "You didn't come when I called you earlier. Now Latha and I are going to play, you can wait your turn."

Maybe it was because Mani was sitting right next to her that Latha lost. "After winning over Mani himself, are you no longer interested in winning a game of pagade, Latha?" Malathi teased.

Latha tried to hide her face further, whispering, "Please be quiet," to Malathi.

This spurred Malathi on to continue teasing and ask, "Ho-ho…it is because Mani is sitting close to you that you have such guts?"

Seeing that Latha was about to get up and run away, Mani said, "Leave it, Akka. Let's you and I play a game."

Just then Malathi's small child woke up and began to cry. "I'll come back in a minute. Until then you both play," Malathi said, and went to put her child back to sleep. That was exactly what Mani wanted too.

The moment Malathi went out of sight, he held Latha's hand and said, "Let's see you run away now."

Latha blushed bright enough to start perspiring. She tried desperately to free her hand. But would Mani let her go! Laughingly, he tried to remove the ring on his finger and put it on hers. Would his ring fit her finger? Finally, he slipped it on her thumb and exclaimed, "How small your fingers are, Latha!"

Latha was leaning close to the ground, bending away out of shyness. Mani had seen her discomfort too. But fearing that she would run away if he left her hand, he held on and said, "What, Latha, are you scared of me?"

Very softly, Latha replied, "No."

"Then why do you run away when you see me?"

Latha did not reply. Mani let her hand go and sat quietly. After a while, Latha said, "I don't want this," removed the ring, kept it in front of Mani and began to get up.

Mani held her hand again, and asked, "Why don't you want it? It is yours after all."

Latha replied, "But I didn't pledge anything on the game."

"Leave it on, Latha. If not winnings from the game, this is an engagement ring then," Mani said and put it back on her thumb.

Latha lifted her head, looked up at Mani's face with a small smile and asked, "Is an engagement ring put on a thumb finger?"

In that tiny smile, Mani got a glimpse into Latha's heart. His chest puffed up with happiness. "I'll get it resized then…?" he asked.

"Hmm," Latha replied.

"Then will you come tomorrow?" Mani asked.

"Hmm," Latha said, and ran away the moment Mani let go of her hand.

After she left, Mani went out into the town. By the time he returned, his ring was smaller in size. The letter 'L' had also joined his initial 'M' on the ring.

The next morning at around ten o'clock, Latha came with four–five roses with the excuse of giving them to Malathi. It was a time when Malathi was very busy in the kitchen. As Latha was returning after giving her the roses, she found Mani standing by the door to his room; he said, "Come here, Latha."

She stood near the door and asked, "What is it?"

Taking the ring out of his pocket, Mani slipped it on her finger, asked, "Now?" and lifted her face by gently tilting her chin. Their eyes met. Again, Mani felt like he had looked into Latha's heart.

5.

That afternoon, Mani got a letter from his friend. "There is a job opening. Come here and try for it," the letter said. Earlier, Mani would have taken a day or two to leave. But now because his marriage to Latha depended on getting a job, he left that very evening. He did not see Latha before leaving. "So what if I don't see her now. She is going to be mine soon," Mani consoled his heart and boarded the train.

Poor thing! How enthusiastically Mani had left! But by the time he reached, that job had gone to somebody else. If not this, some other job; until I find a job, I won't see Latha's face, he told himself and began to roam from place to place looking for work. His heart could not stop thinking about Latha. But the belief that she would be his from the day after he found a job made him forget his weariness, his sadness. Malathi also used to write about Latha. That was why Mani hunted for a job without any worries. But strangely, Mani didn't find a job even eight months after leaving his Akka's place. He took tuition classes here and there to manage his expenses.

In between all this, he began to get letters from Latha's father. "Just get married. Let Latha stay on with us until you get a job," was his opinion. Mani did not want to leave Latha at his in-laws' house just because he couldn't afford to support her. He wrote: "Anyway I am going to marry Latha. So what if that happens after I find a job?"

About three–four days after this, Malathi's letter came. "Rama Rao has got transferred to ___ town. He wants to get Latha married this year itself. Do not be stubborn and wait to get a job. Let her stay at her father's house until you find work," Malathi had written.

Mani wrote back, a bit harshly, that he did not want to get married without a job. He did not get a reply to this letter from either Malathi or from Rama Rao. "Let them get angry. They will get us married off, it is me who has to look after a wife," Mani thought and kept quiet.

Two months went by. Not a single letter from anyone. Meanwhile, he found a job. Though it was not a job befitting his status as the rank holder of a university, he was tired of roaming around and found the work good enough. While he had decided not to write a letter before he heard from them, that very day he wrote to Malathi and Rama Rao to say that he had found a job and he no longer had any objection to the wedding.

Malathi's letter came via the next post itself. He began to read with enthusiasm: by the time the merchant finally got ready, his exalted authority had been looted, as the saying goes.

"Mani, I told you so many times. How long can they keep a grown-up girl at home? Just last week Latha got married, it seems. I got to know through one of your Bhaava's friends. What can be done now? Let what has happened go, we will look elsewhere for a bride for you…" Malathi had written a lot more in the same vein. But Mani did not see any of this. He had lost consciousness by then.

* * *

Six years later, one night Mani had finished dinner and was reading the newspaper. His new bride Lakshmi finished her chores and seeing him sit there reading, came and sat by his feet. As he was reading, Mani held her hand. Five minutes became ten, then fifteen, but it did not look like he had finished reading. Tired of waiting, Lakshmi snatched the paper from his hand. Mani laughed, saying, "You are a shrew, kane," and brought her hand to his lips. But before her hand could reach his lips, he had turned to stone.

Lakshmi asked, "What has happened to my hand?"

Mani had become mute upon seeing the ring on her finger. "Where is this ring from, Lakshmi?" he asked.

Lakshmi laughed and said, "Oh I thought something had happened. Such surprise just for this? This was a present to me from Govinda Rao's wife Latha. They used to live near Anna's house. After Rayaru died, now she is back at her maternal home. She loves me a lot. She sent me the ring in a parcel because she couldn't attend the wedding. See, she has gotten our initials 'M.L.' engraved on it too…" Lakshmi wanted to say much more but stopped, seeing Mani's stunned face and instead asked, "What is it? You are in deep thought?"

"Nothing, just how strange is the game played by fate," Mani replied and sighed deeply.

Though Lakshmi did not understand, she looked at his face and swallowed the question that she wanted to ask.

Her Good Fortune

When Kittanna, who used to adamantly refuse to get married, agreed to marry the village zamindar's daughter…father said yes to the match, thinking it's enough if Kittu gets married and becomes a family man. All the preparations were in full swing. Before anyone could say "haam, hoom," the wedding was already solemnised. What I want to describe now is something that happened during the wedding.

Kittanna and his wife were sitting on the mat for the aarathi-akshate ritual. In the middle of all the chaos of the wedding the previous day, no one had had either the time or the guts to look at the bride and groom properly and tease them. The next day when they were made to sit for the ritual of turmeric and oil smearing, the women had all the freedom. That day, all the married women in the village were present. Never having been the centre of attention of so many women together and being teased by them, Kittanna must have thought, "Enough, enough of this happy married life."

He called me and said, "Somehow ask them to finish this ordeal." But in that kingdom of women, who would pay heed to his words?

"Jaya, sing a song," someone said.

Jaya at first replied "I don't know any," but she was forced to sing.

Tired of sitting, I don't know how Kittanna tolerated the broken tune that came out of her screeching throat. Somehow, her song ended. Saved, I thought. But would one song be enough to finish the ritual? Che, no way, shouldn't at least ten–twenty be sung?

Fine, let them sing however many they want, can't they at least finish it quickly? "You sing, no you sing, no, no, you sing," they would tell each other, then shyly insist that their voice was not alright that day. Then when they started singing (screeching), it would not end even after one hour. Kittanna thought, "If they screech for so long despite having a bad throat, god help us if they were fine." Finally, all the singing ended. Kittanna sat up straight thinking at least now they might do the aarathi and release them.

But that hope lasted just one or two minutes. Two women came holding the aarathi, stood in front of the couple and began debating among themselves: "You sing the song for the aarathi, no, no, you sing…"

Maybe their debating would go on for at least another hour! Sick of this, Kittanna saw a girl sitting next to me and said, "It is okay if they don't know any, you sing a song, girl." Kittanna said so, thinking that this girl who was sitting like a dumb idol would screech a song and stop their debate. I wanted to laugh at Kittanna. This girl singing! If the state of those who sang so far was bad… then this girl….

The girl was about fifteen years old. Her built suggested that she was older. Dark as coal. She had apparently fallen ill a couple of months ago, her hair had fallen out, and was just starting to grow back. Flat nose. Then eyes? I had not seen her eyes, they always lay hidden under her eyelashes. But after seeing her long eyelashes, I had wondered why that unfortunate face needed such beautiful eyelashes. She was Kittanna's father-in-law's watchman's daughter. Poverty, coupled with her poor looks, had made sure she had not found a groom. Nobody liked her very much, though everyone used to say "Paru do this, do that," and make her do all the work. It did not seem like she hated doing all the work. From the day we got there, she had been hovering around me. The way a street dog follows you around if you pat it on the head once. The reason was this: the day we went there, since I did not know anyone, I spoke a few words with her. Since she rarely got to hear kind words, this was enough to win her over. She would bring me whatever I wanted from inside the house; she would follow me around; she would sit near me; like this, not in one but in several ways, she used to display her affection. Her old father, poor man, used to look at her and tease her, saying, "What, dear Paru, will you go away to their town with them?" When she grinned at this, a line of white teeth would flash through that dark face of hers.

Kittanna told her to sing. I also understood what he was thinking and said, "Sing, Paru."

She could not refuse my request. "I don't know an aarathi song. Shall I sing something else?" she asked.

Fearing I might say no, Kittanna quickly said, "It is okay. Sing something."

I also said, "Hmm, sing."

She began to sing—"Paramathma Hare Pavana Naama…."

How many times we have heard that kirthane! That too, in the voices of famous singers! It was true that Paru did not have their experience and technical skill, but that voice, that melody, that power to stir the heart, Paru had infused all these into the kirthane we had heard hundreds of times before. "Paramathma Hare Pavana Naama…"

She continued to sing, unaware of our appreciation. Her eyes, always focused on the ground, were set now upon the skies, as if they were looking at god. Hadn't I called her ugly? What a mad man I am! Aren't her two eyes, like mirrors to her beautiful heart, enough? What an inexcusable stupidity it was that I thought her ugly without having seen those eyes that lent her ordinary face heavenly beauty! Fair skin, long hair, sharp nose, full lips—my feeling that only those who had these were beautiful changed in an instant. Paru's eyes showed me that even inside those who were not outwardly beautiful, there were beautiful hearts. Again, it was Paru's eyes that made me realise that a beautiful heart would not fade away very soon like good looks did and would always remain beautiful.

Where did all of Kittanna's tiredness go? The moment she finished that song, "Sing another," he said.

I had thought that she would offer some excuse saying, "I don't know any, my throat is not alright, enough for now." But there was none of that. The moment Kittanna asked her to sing again, she looked at my face, as if to ask, "Shall I?" Unable to speak, I nodded my head to say yes. She began:

"Nanyaake badavanaiah…"

This was also a kirthane we were bored of listening to hundreds of times. But still when Paru sang it…!

After that song finished, Kittanna wanted to ask her to sing more. It is not that I didn't want that too. But see, she was a poor watchman's daughter. When Kittanna's wife, the zamindar's only daughter, had to play the harmonium and sing for him before giving him tambula, the betel leaf and other things, how could she be given prominence and asked to continue singing?

By the time the tambula, arasina kumkuma and other ritual things were distributed, Paru had left. Though she came the next day, we had to honour invitations to go to the houses of the zamindar's friends and relatives, and did not find the time to get her to sing; in the midst of work, she also didn't have time. Kittanna said several times, "We should get Paru to sing. If she comes, bring her here." But then, like I said, amidst all the bustle of festivities, I couldn't do so. For various reasons, we could not ask her to sing again till we left; we left without hearing her sing again.

She walked till the bus with those who had come to bid us goodbye. When I was boarding the bus, I said, "I will come back, Paru; ask them to send me a card for your wedding."

Her father who was standing right there said, "Will we not send you a card? We are looking, but the time for marriage should also come, after all," and let out a sigh.

Two years later when Kittanna's wife, athige, my sister-in-law went to her mother's place, Paru got married. I had also received an invitation card. But because of various reasons, I was not able to go. Once athige returned, I asked her all about Paru. Athige said, "The poor watchman's ugly daughter got a groom far above her league."

I was not satisfied with only that much. I asked her for details. These were her words— "Yes, she got married. Where would that ugly girl find a suitable groom, tell me? That too without even a paise in dowry. It was her previous life's good fortune. Though he has a bit of tuberculosis, he has enough to provide food and clothes. He took care of all the wedding expenses and married her. In her husband's house, there is no mother-in-law or father-in-law. She only has to take care of the husband a little, she will be well-fed and well-clothed. There is not going to be any impediment to her being happy. Really, Paru is lucky."

The zamindar's only daughter. The wife of a well-earning doctor, Krishnaswamy. Her father's watchman's daughter, no dowry, no other expenses, so what if he has tuberculosis? Is it wrong to think she is fortunate when we see her being married to someone who can provide well for her?

Yes, it is her good fortune!

Kausalyanandana

1.

Anna had written a letter from home: "There is a severe outbreak of small pox here. Do not come home for this vacation, stay there. I will come and pick you up during the Christmas vacation."

Only a week was left before the holidays were to begin. I had looked forward to and yearned for them. All the girls were preparing to go to their villages. I had finished packing my books and clothes before everyone else. Just when I was happily thinking about how I would spend the holidays and what all I would do, came this letter! I had wanted to see Amma, Anna, baby Mohan and others and was sad to see my dreams shatter. Since there was no one in the room, there was no reason for my tears to stop. After all the girls had left, I lay on the bed and worried about how I would spend my days. Just then, Linny came in. Her name was Vasanthi. But when she first joined the school, Vinoda used to tease and call her 'leanie' because she was lean. 'Vasanthi, which Vasanthi?' everyone used to ask. Later on, even the teachers got used to calling her Linny, and the name Vasanthi was forgotten.

Linny was a very smart girl; everyone was her friend. If she had put her mind to it, she could have stood first in class. She would easily finish sums in mathematics that none of us knew anything about. But more than studies, she was interested in playing, in playing pranks. She had a great desire to do what she was told not to. She had been punished several times for climbing the big-big trees in our school compound. There was no one in our school to beat her in tennis and in swimming. Though she was not very beautiful, she had a beautiful voice. During prayer time, listening to her sing made one forget the world. Even girls who were on sick leave would come to listen to her songs during the music period. That was how melodious her voice was. Linny was always merry. None of us had seen her angry or crying. Her nature was always to be up to some prank. It was rare to see her sitting still even for a minute.

She was my roommate. Seeing me lying down, she asked, "What Seetha, have you broken your back? Why are you lying down?"

I giggled, wiped my tears and sat up. She came and sat next to me and asked, "Did you get a letter from home?"

I picked up Anna's letter from the table and gave it to her. After reading it, she said, "Come to our house, Seetha. You always had excuses saying you will come another time. You are not going to your village anyway during this vacation, so come with me. If you say no, I am not going to talk to you."

I was feeling very sad that I had to stay alone after everyone went home. Linny also used to keep inviting me to her house. Thinking that it was better to go with Linny instead of staying alone, I said "Okay."

She was very happy. Though she was friends with all the girls, she had a special affection for me. She was older than me by one year. When the senior girls teased me, Linny always came to my rescue. When everyone got to know that Linny was on my side, the teasing reduced too. The homesickness I had felt when I first came here also reduced thanks to Linny's company. As the days passed, she became closer to me than an older sister. There was nothing I did not share with her. During the last vacation, she had come to my house and stolen Amma's love, Anna's regard and baby Mohan's attachment. No one could stop themselves from loving Linny. All the beautiful qualities that could charm everyone were in my Linny. That was why, even when she was being naughty instead of study-

ing, the Mother Superior would look at her face, not have the heart
to punish her and would forgive Linny instead of reprimanding her.

2.

We left a day earlier than planned. So, there was no one at the
station to pick us up when we got down from the train because
her family did not know we were coming. Linny's house was three
miles away from the station. After the jail-like life we had in the
convent, it was a privilege to go on a leisurely three-mile walk. Linny knew the station master. Though he offered to arrange for a car,
we left our bedding and boxes in his custody and left. Through for-
ests, through plantations, crossing little streams, running and rest-
ing, plucking every wild flower we came across, we did not realise
how quickly we walked the distance and reached Linny's house. It
was nine in the morning. The heat had not risen yet. Her house
was on top of a hill. To get to the house, one had to walk through
a clump of trees and go through the garden. We had reached the
trees. Under one of the trees someone was sitting on a fallen stump
and reading Fitzgerald's "Umar Khayyam" loudly. Since he was sitting with his back to the road, we couldn't see his face. Seeing him,
Linny signalled to me to not make a sound, walked up behind him
softly and covered his eyes with her hands. Startled, he held Linny's hands and whispered, "Vasantha."

Linny laughed, removed her hands and asked, "How did you
know it was me, Ramu?"

"As if I am not acquainted with your hands, is it?" he laughed
and asked, "What Vasantha, why did you lie that you were going
to come tomorrow?"

"Oh, you have started calling me a liar and fighting with me
the minute you see me. The holidays began a day earlier than I expected. If I had waited another day, would I have seen you?"

Linny seemed to have forgotten me in the excitement of
talking to him. I did not want to interrupt them either, so I turned
my back to them and looked down the road that resembled a river

flowing between the trees. Though my eyes were looking at the road, my heart was asking: "Who is this Ramu? Why did Linny never tell me anything about him until today?" I did not know how long I stood there, thinking all this. Seeing a dog run towards me barking, I screamed "Linny!"

Thinking Linny was alone, Ramu turned towards me when I screamed. Immersed in their conversation, Linny also remembered that I was there. She called to the dog, "Teddy, Teddy," patted his head and said, "Ramu, this is my friend Seetha." To me she said, "Seetha, Ramu is one of those mad fellows who reads Omar Khayyam and stories by Kausalyanandana like you."

Those stories and the poems of Omar Khayyam were my favourite. Having gotten to know that Ramu also liked them, I said, "I love them very much."

He smiled and said, "Teasing me by saying that my love for them is a madness is Vasanthi's habit. She never loses a chance to call me mad every opportunity she gets."

"If you two mad people start talking, your conversation will not be over even after it gets dark. Let's go in," Linny said.

Ramu very gently got up with the help of a long stick next to him. I was very surprised to see that one of his legs was shorter than the other.

3.

Ramu was Linny's paternal aunt's son. Having lost both his parents at a young age, he had been raised by Linny's parents. That was why they were so close to each other. It had been decided that Vasantha and he would get married when they were both very young. But he had fallen off a horse when he had gone for his ICS exams and become a cripple; since then her parents had been hesitating to give their daughter in marriage to him. Linny had said firmly, "If I am not marrying Ramu, then I don't want to get married at all." But her parents remained hesitant. That was why Linny's wedding, which was supposed to have happened two years ago, had still not taken place. Ramu had also been feeling awkward since the accident. Thinking that Linny had agreed to marry him only out of pity, he had had a mad thought—that he did not deserve to live at all. Though Linny was in love with Ramu, she had never revealed her feelings in her actions. If she sat down to chat with him, he used to try to hurt her with his words so that at least that way she would stop loving him. Poor Linny used to get very hurt because of his harsh behaviour. When I saw the tears in her eyes that were otherwise always filled with laughter, I would think, "Where is the place for so much love and seriousness in the depths of jolly Linny's heart?" Every time a look of sorrow enveloped Linny's face in her otherwise happy life, I used to feel anger towards Ramu. Several times I thought I should ask him, "Why are you doing this?" But if Linny got to know that I had asked him this....I kept quiet thinking of the consequences.

It was the day of the half-moon rising. As decided the previous day, we all got ready to go to the river to bathe. If we walked, it would be late by the time we had our baths and came back since the river was far away. So, it was decided that we would go in the car, and Ramu could also come. Linny, her parents and I tried our best to get Ramu to come with us. But he did not agree. Seeing this, Linny also changed her mind, "I will not come," was her answer to everyone. The previous day, she had happily believed that Ramu might accompany them. Seeing how dejected she now was, I felt uncontrollable anger towards Ramu. "What qualities does she see in this egotistical cripple that she loves him so much!" I fumed. The more I thought about it, the more I felt that Ramu was not the right match for my Linny. When I saw how she went against her parents' wishes and even tolerated Ramu's constant rejection of her love, I decided that love was truly blind.

Linny loved swimming. Every time we went for a picnic to the river from school, the teachers would have a hard time trying to make her come out of the water. I had thought that all the sadness she was feeling when leaving home would be forgotten the minute Linny saw the river. But even after reaching the river, she did not show much enthusiasm like I had expected. The girl who used to swim like a fish when she saw water finished her bath in five minutes and came out to the river bank. I could not tolerate the thought of Linny sacrificing herself to that cripple's ego. I decided to tell him off soundly as soon as we got back home.

4.

If I had known the consequences of the decision I had made for the sake of Linny, for her happiness and out of my love for her, I would never have attempted to berate Ramu. How would I have known, that as a result of my scolding, Ramu would leave home to wander the country! If I had known earlier that what I did to try and help her would destroy even the little happiness she had, I would not have said those hurtful words to Ramu. But, if the future could be known, so many changes in the world would have come to pass easily.

Though in retrospect I think this now, I believed that what I did earlier was right. That day, the harsh words I had uttered while asking for Linny's happiness were truly hurtful to Ramu. If not, Ramu—simple hearted Ramu—was not stonehearted enough to have left that night under the darkness of the new moon, without telling anyone, casting away the security and love of the aunt and uncle who had raised him and who were dearer to him than his own parents.

Though I had wanted to do good by Linny, I ended up harming her. No one knew the reason Ramu had left. I did not have the courage to tell anyone either. Every time I saw Linny's wilted face, it was like a gash to my heart. What would she say if she knew the consequence of having taken me to her house as a dear friend! My heart trembled thinking of it, thinking of the possibility of losing Linny's friendship. My bravado to confess my mistake kept taking a step back.

We returned to the school when there were still two days of holidays left. None of the other girls had returned, just us two. Though every moment spent with Linny was precious to me, I was scared to look at her face after having extinguished the light in her life because of my stupidity. After the holidays, when all the girls returned, they noted Linny's lack of humour and naughtiness, her serious face, shrunken eyes and her desire to be alone, with surprise and asked me, "Seetha, what happened to Linny?"

What could I say? As the days passed by, Linny left aside all her earlier games, fun, laughter and studied all the time. She was now the teachers' favourite student. She stood first in class. She was completely different from the Linny before the vacations. Earlier, her habit was to keep talking after the lights were switched off at night. But now she would go to bed the minute she came into the room. Though I knew she had not fallen asleep, I could not gather the courage to talk to her. Though we stayed in the same room, towards the end, it became rare for us to speak even one word.

One night, we had switched off the lights and lay on our beds. Neither of us was asleep. "Seetha," Linny called. It had been many days since we had talked. Hearing her call my name, I remembered our old days, our friendship, and burst out crying. Though I tried to control myself, I could not. I began to sob uncontrollably. Yet, I did not find the courage to admit my mistake. Hearing me weep, Linny got up, held my hands and said, "Seetha, my Seetha, forgive me."

"Forgive you?" It was I who had to fall at her feet and beg for her forgiveness. For what crime should the simple-hearted Linny ask my forgiveness? She started talking again, "Though I don't chatter away with you like I used to, you are a dearer friend to me than earlier Seetha. Even my mother does not know the depths of my heart like you do. Seetha, there is a reason for my behaviour to have caused you sorrow. But you are closer to me than you were earlier Seetha. Seetha…Seetha…."

Linny began to sob her heart out. I did not know how to console her. I hugged her, laid her head on my shoulder and began to weep silently.

5.

One year went by. We finished our high school education as well. Since my father was an advocate of women's education, he decided to send me to college. If Linny had desired to study further, her parents would not have stopped her. But she decided to stay at home. After being together for nine years, we found it very difficult when the time for separation came. I suffered a lot of anguish when I thought of her future life. But still I did not find the courage to tell her the reason why Ramu had left home. I decided to write a letter and beg for her forgiveness after reaching Madras, and left without telling her the reason. Since Anna got transferred to Madras the year I went there, I did not have to live in a hostel and went to college from home.

After we set up home in Madras, I wrote several letters to Linny asking her to come stay with us for a few days. She kept giving one or the other reason for not being able to visit. Thinking that I would tell her when she came to stay with us, I still had not told Linny the reason why Ramu had decided to wander the country. After she wrote that she was not going to come, I decided I would go to her place. But I could not go during that vacation because Mohan had fallen ill. His illness completely changed my life. Aruna Devi, the doctor who used to come to treat him, was from Kannada land. By the time Mohan recovered, a friendship had developed between her and me. As per her advice, I decided to sit for a medical exam after my FA. Since my parents did not object, after eight years of study, I passed my MBBS exam and became a doctor. Though I kept writing letters to Linny for all those eight years, I could not meet her. She also had not come to our house. From her letters I knew that she was of the opinion to never get married at all. That I was the reason for this kept nagging my heart.

After the bustle of my exams, I left for her house once I was free. The old place, the same path, the same old house. But what a difference between going then and going there now! What difference between that Linny and the Linny now! I was the reason for this. In the last several years, Linny's life had undergone a complete change. She knew that it was impossible to see Ramu. Peace had now replaced the hope that used to flash across her face that she would see him again. While earlier she would sit still and think about him, now she would do some work and try to forget him. After her chores when she got some free time, she would read stories written by Kausalyanandana. Earlier she used to laugh at us for reading them, calling us mad, and now she had grown very fond of them. If I asked, she said, "When I read the stories of Kausalyanandana, I get a kind of peace, Seetha. When I am feeling sad, reading them makes me feel better." There really was that power in his books. His newly published book "Vasantha Kusuma" was such that no one who read it could forget his stories.

I had made up my mind when I left home that I simply had to tell Linny that I was the reason why Ramu had gone away. One night before I was to return, when we were sitting in the full moon light under the mango tree at the end of the veranda, I told her everything and begged for her forgiveness.

"Seetha, what is the use of worrying about what has happened, tell me? Why do you ask me to forgive you? You know that I am not angry with you. Do not bring up this subject again."

After telling Linny and asking for her forgiveness, I felt as relieved as if I had put down a heavy load. I did not have the courage to look at her face and talk to her. The next day when I left, Linny also came home with me.

6.

Eight days went by since Linny came home. I took her to Dr Aruna Devi's house to introduce them to each other. When we went, she was sitting alone, sewing. She was very happy to meet Linny. Aruna

Devi was very fond of music. When two music lovers meet, what could I, who knew not a whiff of music, talk to them about! I sat at a table in a corner and began to read one of Kausalyanandana's books. Seeing me pick up that book, Aruna Devi said, "Seetha, Anna and Kausalyanandana came by the train this morning. They have gone out somewhere now. If you stay till seven, you can meet your favourite author."

Both Linny and I had long wanted to meet Kausalyanandana, and we were happy to have an opportunity to see him.

Wondering how long they would take to come back, I flipped through the pages of the book restlessly. Aruna Devi had placed a harmonium before Linny and was asking her to play. When Linny began to play the harmonium and sing, I closed the book and began to listen, forgetting everything else. Aruna Devi sat there like a statue, listening to Linny as if she was under a spell. That was how melodious Linny's voice was. The song she was singing was that meaningful too—Laila and Majnu's love song. Since I knew Linny's life very well, tears began to flow from my eyes when she sang that enchanting song in her honeyed voice. Aruna Devi also sat there, stunned, unmindful of the tears that flowed down her face as well.

Linny's song ended. Having been immersed in a world of feelings, we came back to our senses. Aruna Devi held Linny's hands and said, "Though I had heard from Seetha that you sing very well, I would not have even dreamed that you sing this exquisitely."

Linny replied, "I have not touched the harmonium in a long time. I have lost the touch of playing it," and got up. Linny's humbleness completely won over Aruna Devi.

We had lost track of time because of Linny's singing. The clock showed that it was seven. Kausalyanandana had not yet come. We said we would return the next day and left. When we got to the portico, we saw them both sitting outside. Since it was dark, we couldn't see their faces. Aruna asked, "Anna, what time did you come?"

He replied, "We came an hour ago. Fearing that the singing would stop and we wouldn't get the privilege to listen, we did not come inside and sat out here."

Aruna Devi turned to Linny, told him that she was the singer and said, "This is my brother, and this is Kausalyanandana."

By then one of the domestic helps had placed a lamp outside. We saw in the light…what a tremendous surprise! The beloved Kausalyanandana of Kannadigas—Ramu who had stolen Linny's heart!

Linny said, "Ramu", with surprise, with happiness.

Forgetting that we were all there, Ramu took her hands in his and said, "My Vasantha!"

Paapa's Wedding

If I begin to think of the games, the fun and the fights of those days, I feel like laughing. May that childhood come back just once more. Back then, we only wished to grow up quickly so that we could escape all the torture. Now we lament for the happy childhood that is over. Though our childhood is over, the friendship from those young days has only grown. 'Paapa' has finished his college education and is now a lawyer. Me!? Famous back then for being naughty, I am now the mother of a naughty boy. If I complain when Baby is being naughty, Akka still makes fun, saying, "You think you were any better?"

1.

Paapa and I grew up together. He is my elder sister's son—more than the blood relationship, ours is a bond of friendship. When we were children, we used to fight often. We would stop talking to each other. But all that would only last one second; in the very next instant, we would forget about the fight and start playing together again. He must be younger than me by one or two years. Based on that one–two years of seniority, it was my desire that he should do what I tell him to. Suppose he said, "Hmm, I won't" for anything I told him, that was it, I would give him a nice beating. He would cry and run inside to complain to the elders. Either Akka or Amma would come out asking me why I hit Paapa and give me a punch on my back. I would get angry and refuse to let Paapa join me in playing. It was true that Paapa could not bear the pain from my beatings and went inside to complain. But after I myself got punched in the back, his pain would reduce a bit and he would stop crying. He would want to start playing like before. But fresh from having been punched and angry that he had got me beaten, I would refuse to play with him. The angrier I got, the softer Paapa became. In the end, he would give me the chalk, marble and peppermint from his pocket and call a truce. We would begin to play cheerfully again. This was chapter one in our daily routine.

The second chapter was our bath. If we got to know that the elders were going to give us an oil bath, that was it, we would go and hide somewhere. We could not escape the bath though, no matter where we hid. They would search all corners, drag us out and apply oil on us. After that, I would say, "Let Paapa bathe first" and he would say, "Let hers be first." It would be like a big war. The reason was this; we could play in the mud a little longer than the one who was bathed first. In between this, the oil would drip down from the head and fall into the eyes. We would wipe it away with our muddy hands and when the eyes started burning, we would cry, "Bathe me first." Me first, me first was another fight. If all this ended, another would begin about where we would sit to have lunch. Akka would come, give us a whack and make us sit in our places. After that it was, "The small stool for me, for me." After that, "You must serve me first, no me first." After this ended and we began eating lunch, Paapa would bite into a chilly and scream "Aiyooo kaaaraaa." By the time he was given water and calmed down, I would have some complaint. With all this, by the time we finished lunch, at least one hour would have gone by. After lunch we would take a nap for at least an hour. Though we didn't want to, Akka would threaten us with a stick, "Are you going to sleep or not?" and we had to sleep, for fear of the stick. When Anna, Murthy and everyone else could do what they wanted, we wondered why we had to sleep. But the stick in Akka's hand would make us stay quiet and close our eyes. The minute we closed our eyes, Akka would leave to finish chores inside. The instant Akka turned her back, we would open our eyes and sit up. But we did not have the guts to go play outside.

During the holidays we would see Anna and Murthy play cards in the afternoon. It was the only game we knew that could be played sitting down. But we needed cards. So what? Anna's book was on the table. We could tear off its pages. This was my suggestion. Paapa did not approve. My idea was that Paapa should tear the pages and bring them, in case someone found out and blamed me. Okay, the game was about to begin. Pages with pretty-pretty dolls were for me, but Paapa was the one who tore them off—would he be quiet? He said he wanted the nice-looking doll pictures. This fight would go on until Akka came and gave us a whack. We had to sleep again. This time angry with each other, we would not talk and sleep. As if on cue, we would fall asleep too. By the time we woke up, coffee and snacks would be ready. Though we would have forgotten what we had fought about before we slept, we would start fighting again without fail during snack time, just like we had done during lunch.

After this, we would start playing in the front yard. About this time, the snacks in Paapa's pocket would fall into my stomach; once the snacks were finished, he would start crying. Akka would come and shout at me and give him more snacks. By the time he came to a truce with me, those snacks would again be mine. By then, it would be around six in the evening. The event of washing our hands and legs would begin. Again, a small fight. By the time this was getting over, our teacher would arrive. We wondered where he came from! If he came, that was it, there was no end to our misery. Sleep and thirst, like never before, would come upon us. Once in a while, we would get stomach ache too. Though we would get out of lessons initially saying we had stomach ache, later on, the teacher would use the stick to cure us of our aches. Every evening we used to crib, "It would be so nice if our master was not there." But the more we wished death and fever upon him, the healthier and stronger he became.

Our brother used to write poetry. His habit was to make us all sit around and read what he had written to us. We also composed a poem to show we were equal to him. "If the bloody master died…" began our poem. Thinking that we wrote a poem only to make fun of him, Anna snatched the paper from our hands and showed it to master that evening. We were done for then; our backs had blisters from the caning we received. We stopped writing poetry from that day onward.

Another day. We were going to school by then. Which also meant that we had a little more freedom. In our heads we were now equal to Anna and Murthy and were proud of it. When both of them could ride a bicycle, why we could not do it too was a question that bothered us for many days. When we got a chance, could we let it go? Claiming seniority, I insisted on climbing on the bicycle first. Paapa agreed too. Using a stool and with Paapa's help, I climbed on the bicycle. But…you can imagine what happened next! Both my knees split open and blood gashed out. On the one hand there was pain and on the other hand the worry that we would be scolded if the elders got to know. Paapa had gone mute with fear seeing the blood gushing out from my knees. I was also not in a state to get up from where I had fallen. I had assumed that I would get a lot of beatings that day. But seeing the state I was in, no one said anything. 'You should not do naughty things like this and get hurt," they all said, gently. 'Thank god no one scolded me," I thought to myself with relief, and let go of the desire to ride a bicycle from that day. Paapa though did not stop at this, and somehow learnt to ride. But even today when I think of the bicycle ride of that day, a shiver runs down my spine.

It took fifteen days for the wounds to heal. Even then, I could not walk properly. My mother feared that I might have broken a bone. The doctor said it was not so, and that there was only a sprain somewhere. Bhageerathamma was called to set the sprain right. Bhageerathamma was an unfortunate old woman; she would beg in a few houses and fill her stomach. Everyone said that she was very good at removing sprains and cramps. When she came begging the next day, my mother asked her to set my sprain right, and that if she was successful, she would be given a saree. From that day onward, hell began for me.

When Bhageerathamma poured oil and massaged my leg to remove the sprain, it felt like my life was slipping away. If I shouted in pain, everyone would scold me, saying, "Who asked you to try to ride the bicycle? If you don't keep quiet and sit still now, you will become lame." I also wanted to heal quickly and escape from having to be house-bound. Finally, after Bhageerathamma's great massages, my leg became all right after seven or eight days. She also got a saree.

A week or two after this, I don't know what happened, Bhageerathamma passed away. She died, and there was no one to cry for her. But from the day she died, Paapa and I were greatly troubled. We had heard ghost stories from our maids and from Anna and Murthy. But since no one in our village had died recently, we did not fear ghosts much. We felt very strange when we got to know that it was Bhageerathamma who had died, the one who used to come to our house for alms every day, and who had recently healed my leg. To top this, our maid was talking to someone about her and we heard her say, "She had not even worn the new saree the lady of our house had given her. Wonder what special occasion she was saving it for!" We had heard that if someone greatly desired something, they would come back after death as ghosts. The maid's words made us feel that Bhageerathamma was really going to turn into a ghost. We talked about this throughout the day. At night we got all kinds of scary dreams. We got a little courage once morning arrived. At night, we needed company to go from one room to the other. Akka, Amma and everyone else used to get angry seeing this behaviour of ours. "She died somewhere and has become dust, you are behaving like mad people," they said.

No matter what anyone said, our fear of Bhageerathamma did not reduce. When our maid told us how after she finished work and went past Bhageerathamma's hut on her way home, she saw a light inside the hut, we decided that she had really turned into a ghost. No matter how much Paapa and I fought during the day, by nightfall we would have reconciled. We needed each other's company if Bhageerathamma's ghost came. Anna and Murthy also strengthened our belief. If we did not do what they told us to, they would say, "Wait till nightfall, we will make the ghost come."

"Will it come just for us? It will come for you too," Paapa told them once.

They said, "We have had the upanayana ceremony, we have the janivaara, the sacred thread around us. If we show the janivaara, it won't do anything." They used fear to get us to do things for them. This way, a month or two passed. Maybe because we were doing chores for the janivaara-clad Anna and Murthy, our fear of Bhageerathamma began to diminish every passing day. The fact that we had not laid eyes on Bhageerathamma's ghost even so many days after her death was another reason.

2.

One Sunday, while returning from the women's association, I went to Seetha Bai's house. It was around half past five in the evening. I would have stayed there another half an hour, but Maada came running to say that someone had come home and that I should come back immediately. Wondering who it might be, I hurried back. It was Paapa. It had been a long time since we had met. I was very happy to see him. "Such a rare thing you have become," I remarked.

"What can I do, Aunty, I don't get any time at all," he replied.

"Anyway, at least you got time now," I said.

"I have delegated all my work to Raja Rao and made myself free for four days; I have no desire to go anywhere now, there is too much work. But I cannot bear Amma's stubbornness. All day long her only chant is that I should take you along for another exhibition. She won't come this time it seems," he said.

Well, the reason why Paapa had come was now clear. I had to go with him this time. It was only going and coming back, Paapa was not going to agree. "Why spend money to simply go and come back? You won't approve anyone," I said.

Paapa replied, "What do I do, Aunty? If I don't go, Amma will get hurt. As for me, when I see all this, I feel like I don't want marriage or anything. Amma just wants a daughter-in-law to come, no matter what. But then see, am I not the one who has to experience marriage? How can I be happy if I marry some uneducated village girl? Now too we are to go to the house of a Jois, the village astrologer. I have met the Jois. After seeing him, there is no need at all to see his daughter, that is the way he is. What can I do, Aunty? I cannot tolerate Amma's pressure. How can I say no without meeting the girl, she says, so I thought I will see her and say no."

I agreed with Paapa. He was an educated boy. It was natural that he wanted an educated, good-looking girl. How could he be forced to marry a village girl who would not have a clue of urban life? Akka was old-fashioned, all she wanted was a daughter-in-law in the house. She would have liked it better if the girl was old-fashioned as well. Unfortunately, there were few educated girls in our community. If there was a girl who had studied a little bit, she wouldn't be too good looking. "Why do I have to get married within our own community? What is the problem if she is from some other Brahmin community?" Paapa would ask.

How would Akka be okay with this? We had all decided that Paapa would only get married the day the eternal bachelor god Ganesha got married.

We left by bus at seven the next morning. When I asked Paapa what time we would reach, he replied that we might reach by evening. It became evening but we had not yet reached the village. By around half past six we came to a village, not the one we wanted though. The bus would leave that place only the next morning at eight o'clock. It was the first time we had come to that village. We did not know anyone. There were no good hotels there either.

Thankfully I had left Baby at home and come. We had to somehow spend the night there. The next afternoon we would reach the Jois's house. But where to spend the night? "Let's go check at the Traveller's Bungalow," Paapa said. We got a coolie to carry our trunks and bedding.

The TB was one and a half miles from the bus stand. When it was so hard to find someone to carry our luggage, there was no question of finding a vehicle. We walked all the way. We had had nothing to eat since morning. It felt like our legs were dead after sitting on the bus all day. By the time we reached the TB, it was eight o'clock. I wondered which unlucky stars were shining when we left the house! "The District Commissioner has come and camped here, there are no rooms available," they told us. We walked back to the village the same way we had come. By then the clock had struck nine. We were both hungry and very tired from having travelled all day. In between all this, our coolie was grumbling that he was getting late. After enquiring all over the village, a kind man finally told us we might get space to stay at the municipal office. By the time we got there, the peon had shut the doors and gone home. We then went to his house. By the time he came and opened the office for us, the clock was striking eleven. After this, our coolie started fighting saying that the money we gave him was not enough. Finally, by half past eleven all of this was resolved and we just wanted to go to sleep. We spread the bedding and went to sleep By the time we woke up it was morning. When we had folded the bedding and washed our faces, the bus had come. If it was his own house, if the coffee was not ready when he woke up, Paapa would grumble, "What is this Amma, the coffee is still not ready." Here! Where was there coffee in this godforsaken village! We were so used to drinking coffee that we felt strange without it. What else could we do, by afternoon we would reach the Jois's house, and till then we had to be quiet.

The bus started. This road was worse than the one we had travelled on the previous day. We hoped our bones wouldn't break by the time we reached the Jois's house. Paapa, irritated, said, "Thoo, if I knew all this would happen, who would have come? I have had enough of this seeing girls and everything else."

"Do you think marriage is a simple thing, Paapa? You will forget all this tiredness the minute you meet the girl. Only I am needlessly roaming around like this," I teased. "Ayyo, be quiet, Aunty. I am fed up even before seeing the girl, god help me after seeing her," Paapa said, grinning.

We reached the village by around one o'clock that afternoon. Now we had to look for their house. We had not told them that we were coming. If they were informed, Paapa believed that we wouldn't get to see the girl properly. "See Aunty, if they know we are going, they will decorate the girl like a doll with make-up before meeting us. We can't make out her skin colour also," he said.

"You refuse a girl before even meeting her. What do you care what she looks like?" I asked.

"After taking all this trouble to come here, shouldn't I at least see the girl once?" Paapa said. He won. We did not inform them of our visit.

It was a very small village. It must have been very rare that they had new visitors. The moment we got off the bus, people began to stare at us as if we were strange creatures. "Do we have horns or have they never seen human beings that they are looking at us like this," Paapa grumbled.

"How do we look like regular people to them, Paapa, especially you, with your suit, looking like a sahib," I said.

Finally, after getting someone to carry our luggage and enquiring here and there, we found the Jois's house. His house was near the village temple. There was a festival that day at the temple. After all the rituals were completed, the Brahmins were sitting on the steps of the temple chewing paan. The Jois was also there. A lot of devotees used to come to that village during this festival. Hence our arrival did not cause much curiosity. They must have thought we were also devotees from somewhere. Until we got closer, the

Jois must have thought that too. Once we got closer, his darling son-in-law to-be! His joy knew no bounds. "Oh, you have come! You did not inform us at all. Lo, Ranga, go get two pots of water… tell someone to get some juice to quench their thirst…," he went about excitedly. His hospitality made us forget our long, inconvenient journey.

We had to go past the temple to reach his house. After a round of hospitality at the temple, the Jois took us along to his house. A boy stood at the door; it must have been his son, aged about sixteen or seventeen. The Jois addressed him, "Lo, spread out a mat and tell someone to heat water for a bath. These people haven't had a bath yet."

The boy also seemed to have thought we were devotees visiting the temple. He called out, "Lakshmi, bring a mat and come," and immediately Lakshmi brought out a mat and began spreading it out.

That was the first time I saw Lakshmi. Paapa saw her too. Maybe if he knew she was the Jois's daughter whom we had come to meet, he would have looked at her properly. But he did not know that.

You might wonder how I got to know. I guessed because I already knew from Akka's letter that the girl whom Paapa was to meet was named Lakshmi. That is why I looked at her, and silently prayed to god, "Let this girl be Paapa's."

You might ask how I could have guessed all her virtues and faults just by looking at her once. I don't have the strength to reply to that. If I was asked if Lakshmi was a very good-looking girl, I would have to say no. If she were to be compared to the beauties in Ravi Varma paintings, then Lakshmi was not a very beautiful girl. Neither was she ugly, in case you wondered. Then you might wonder what else I saw and got attracted.

The answer to that is this: there was something very attractive about Lakshmi. If I am asked what that means, I am not capable of describing her beauty. Her charm cannot be reduced to words. But all I can say is, even if someone saw her just once, they would not forget her face for many days. Lakshmi spread the mat and went inside. We sat down on the mat. Poor fellow! The Jois was flustered. We had come without giving him notice. It seemed like he didn't have many facilities at home because of his work at the temple. He was worried we might take offence or be disappointed. He ended every other sentence saying, "Oh, this is a poor family's house."

We felt sorry looking at his self-deprecating manner. Such humility towards a potential bridegroom in spite of having a daughter like Lakshmi! Should someone bend over backwards with others just for having girl children, I wondered. Paapa also hesitated to accept his hospitality. The minute he went in, Paapa asked, "What is this! Am I already his son-in-law? Why so much of ceremony!"

"So what if you are not his son-in-law yet? You definitely will be, going ahead," I laughed.

"What, Aunty, am I going to marry his daughter, or him!?" Paapa asked.

"Oh you haven't stopped your jest yet. The girl who brought out the mat, that's her…," I said.

"Oh that girl is it…" when Paapa was dragging out his thought, the Jois came out just then saying that hot water was ready for our baths.

By the time the Jois had returned, everyone in the house had got to know why we had come. Everyone was ready to please us. His wife came to take me inside for a bath. That boy, the young astrologer Joshi took Paapa. We finished our bath and lunch comfortably. Then the Jois couple indicated that we should have a nap and recover from our journey. By the time we got up, coffee and snacks were ready. After we had our coffee, the Jois took us along for a stroll. By the time we walked to the village's Hanumantha shrine and got back, it was dark. Along the way if one of his acquaintances asked who we were, he would smile and give them our entire history, and end by saying, "They have come to see Lakshmi."

Paapa was very irritated with his enthusiasm. "What is this! Have I come to meet the girl or to exhibit myself?" he grumbled to me.

How was the Jois to know that we disliked this kind of boasting? He was beaming with pride. We finally reached home by the time it was dark.

The Jois washed his hands and feet and sat down for his japa meditation. Paapa also finished his evening prayer ritual for appearance's sake. Then, as usual, dinner. In spite of all this, we had seen Lakshmi only once when she had come out in the afternoon to lay the mat. She was nowhere to be seen after getting to know the reason we had come. After the men finished dinner and stepped out, I asked her mother, "Where is Lakshmi? She is nowhere to be seen."

Her mother said, "She is very shy. She has been in the prayer room since afternoon." She called out "Come Lakshmi, there is no one here," and Lakshmi came in, very hesitantly.

I saw her face and prayed to god, "Make Paapa agree to this match."

She came and sat next to me for dinner. I began to talk to her during dinner. "Do you know how to cook, Lakshmi?"

"A little," she said.

"Till which grade have you studied?" I asked.

"I have passed primary school,"

"Do you know music?"

"Just a very little bit."

We spoke about this and that. By the time we finished dinner, her initial shyness had disappeared and she began talking to me with ease. She had finished eating before me. By the time I had washed my hands and come back in, she was standing near the window and looking at Paapa who was seated on the sit-out outside. She must have felt very shy seeing me there. She tried running inside the prayer room. I held her hand and teased, "Why are you running away?"

She was embarrassed to have been caught looking at Paapa and managed to escape.

The next morning after coffee, Paapa said, "What, Aunty, have we come here only to be treated to their hospitality? Tell them we have to leave this afternoon itself."

"But Paapa, you have come to meet the girl. How can we go without finishing the job we came for?" I asked him.

At that moment the Jois came there with a new person. The new face belonged to the Jois's neighbour Shasthri. "I am very happy to meet you. Did you like our girl?" he asked, grinning wide.

"The one who has to like her has not yet met her," I said, grinning back.

"Is that so? Joisre, call Lakshmi. Let her play some harmonium," he said.

There the Jois went inside the house, and here Shasthri started singing his praises. "Let me marry the Jois itself, after hearing all these praises," Paapa mumbled.

The litany of good things about the Jois continued until Lakshmi came out. The young boy brought out the harmonium and placed it in front of her. Shastri stopped talking about the Jois and proceeded to rave about Lakshmi's virtues. Poor thing! As it is that girl was very shy. She could barely lift her face up. "Play Raghuvamsha Sudha, my dear. Sing along too," said the Shasthri.

Lakshmi began to play.

It did not look like she had a lot of practice in music. But her voice was very sweet; one did not feel like saying enough, stop, while listening to her sing.

One after the other, Shasthri made her sing four or five songs. During all this, Paapa who had come to meet her was looking not at her, but elsewhere. I was very amused looking at him, but controlled my laughter.

Lakshmi finished singing. The Jois went in for some reason. Shasthri asked her to sing another song. She had been singing without a break for half an hour; alongside were her hesitancy, fear and to top it off, her shyness. Was this a bride test or a grave punishment, I wondered.

"That is enough, Shasthrigale," I said, and told Lakshmi, "You sing very well, my dear."

Lakshmi was just about to get up when Shasthri said, "These people want to hear you read something. Show them how you read."

Lakshmi went in to get a book. Paapa did not open his mouth and kept quiet, looking elsewhere. I remembered everything he had said during our journey, and could not control my laughter. He had said, "The girl should answer all my questions. She should say whether she wants to marry me or not. If she is shy and behaves like someone old-fashioned, I will certainly say no."

I had shut him up saying, "Anyway you have already decided you will say no without even seeing her. Good if she is shy, you will have a reason to refuse the match."

But now forget asking her questions, Paapa was hesitating to even look in her direction.

Lakshmi got a book and started reading. I cannot remember now what it was but she read very well. As her reading was about to end, Shasthri went out to spit out the betel leaves and nut he had stuffed in his mouth.

It was the best time for Paapa to ask her something. I pinched him and indicated that he should talk to her. He, who was capable of confusing scores of witnesses in court with his cross questioning, did not seem able to even talk at that moment, for some reason. I pinched him harder. Unable to bear the pressure, just as Paapa managed to bring his gaze from elsewhere and turn towards Lakshmi, she finished her reading and lifted her head up, and their eyes met. Lakshmi dropped her head down the very next second. Her face was flushed. Paapa's eyes did not turn elsewhere. I pinched him softly again. With a faint smile he looked at me and whispered, "This is not as easy as questioning a witness in court, Aunty."

Hearing us both laugh softly, Lakshmi must have thought we were laughing at her, and began to rise from her seat. Fearing that she was about to leave, Paapa said, "Why are you leaving. Please sit down."

When she sat down, there started Paapa's barrage of questions. Though he asked, "What's your name," first, he of course knew her name. But he needed something easy to start with.

I had thought Lakshmi might be too shy to answer. But she answered with a serious face, "Seethalakshmi."

I was happy that she was talking. "How old are you?" was Paapa's second question.

"Fifteen," pat came her reply.

"What class have you studied up to?" to this third question came her answer,

"I have passed fourth standard."

"Do you know how to cook?" This was the fourth question.

When she replied, "I can cook a little," Paapa retorted, "If you want to eat well, you should learn to cook well."

"What is this, Paapa is already issuing orders to her!" I thought, surprised. But I was happy thinking that this must mean he liked her.

Paapa's fifth question was, "Do you agree to marrying me?"

She did not answer. "Then you don't agree?"

When Paapa asked his sixth question, his voice was anxious. She very softly said, "I agree."

The smile that had vanished from Paapa's face was back again. "Our village is very far away. Won't be you upset to leave your parents and live there?" he asked.

"So what if it is far, I'll get used to it," she said.

"You sang very well, Lakshmi. But when I come the next time, you should learn to sing even better…"

"Okay, I'll learn," Lakshmi replied.

"Do you know how to write letters?" Uff, Paapa is one smart boy, I thought.

She said, "Yes, I know."

"Then will you write to me?" She did not reply. "Leave it, if not to me, will you write to Aunty at least?"

"Hmm." I wonder what else Paapa wanted to ask her. But Shasthri came back and he became silent. Lakshmi got up. This time Paapa did not stop her.

Paapa agreed. What else did we have to do here, we could leave that afternoon, I thought. "Shall we leave in the afternoon, Paapa?" I asked.

But I wonder why, he said, "Let us leave tomorrow, aunty."

Vani's Puzzle

1.

That morning when Indu woke up and came out of her house, it looked like there were new tenants in the house next door that had been vacant for many years. There was a truck in front of the house and voices coming from inside. More than being curious about who was moving in—the house had remained vacant for five-six years—Indu was sad. She was not of the nature to think "if the grandma in the neighbouring house dies, we'll have space to tie the calf there." But to say that she was more aggrieved than was pleased about someone coming to live next door would not be wrong. There was a reason for her to feel that way.

Indu lost her father before she was born, her mother when she was born and grew up as a burden to everyone in a relative's house. As if this was not enough, she was allotted widowhood within six months of being married. The small house she was living in now was the only reminder that she had been married once, a long time ago. When he got to know that it was impossible for him to live any longer, her husband transferred the house and some money to her name, and Indu was able to live without being dependent on others.

She loved her house very much. Her goal in life was to keep it beautiful. Having grown up without a place for "me" or "mine", it was no surprise that she had so much love for the house. Also, if she had seen any happiness in life, it was in that house. Before she was even old enough to understand that her life would be ruined if he died, her husband had passed away. After seeing his face during the wedding, the next time she saw his face was after he had died. Actually, it must be said that her life was a little happier only after he died. Greedy for the money her husband had bequeathed her, the love for her increased among members of her family. But once Indu was old enough to understand things, she desired to live by herself, independently. If not for her sake, but for the love of her wealth, her family had said several times, "It is not right for a young woman like you to live alone in a house." But Indu had not changed her decision.

This was six years ago. Then she had been twenty years old. When she left her village and came to this house, the house next door had been vacant. From that day till now, it had become customary for Indu to go to the backyard next door with the same freedom with which she roamed in her own backyard. She hadn't even found it necessary to repair the fence in the middle that the passage of time had broken.

Hers was a soul that liked solitude. Having grown up alone without ideas of "her own" and "hers", after becoming independent she did not see the need for the company, friendship and love of others. Even if she felt the need, it was not in her reserved nature to seek the friendship of others. So, it was no surprise that having been by herself for so long, it did not make her happy to find that there were new tenants next door. It was not that her happiness was dependent on whether there were people next door or not. Even if she knew that, she couldn't help feel, "oh, someone has come." Thinking that if she didn't get the fence repaired now, her privacy would suffer, Indu went inside and did not go to the backyard again that day.

2.

The next day when Indu was getting the fence repaired, she saw a woman her age near the well in the backyard of the house next door. She also saw Indu, and smiled. The reflection of that smile beamed on Indu's face too. Even though there was two days' worth of work left, after that day, the repair work on the fence did not continue.

This way, the acquaintance of Indu and the neighbour Vani started with a smile and found its way to friendship by the time a week had passed. Having had no desire for anyone's friendship, it surprised Indu to feel affection for Vani grow in her. Vani was new to the town, she did not know anyone there. Every day as morning dawned, she would see Indu's face. So, it did not surprise Vani that her acquaintance with Indu had turned into friendship. But never having known such a natural friendship before, that this feeling would be mirrored in her heart was what Indu did not expect.

Vani lived with her husband Ratna, who was newly transferred to the town as the doctor. Since he was the only doctor in town, he was always very busy and often did not even find time to eat. Vani found it boring to stay home by herself, so three quarters of her time was spent in Indu's house. Indu had visited her a couple of times too.

The very first time Indu went to Vani's house, clothes, utensils and kitchen things were scattered all around. Even though Vani said, "It is because we have recently moved in that I have not had the time to arrange everything properly," Indu, who always maintained her house immaculately thought, "Even fifteen days after coming, you didn't find time?" with surprise.

That day she assisted Vani in sorting everything. They started work at two o'clock in the afternoon, but by the time they finished everything it was almost dark. When everything was done, the house looked clean and beautiful.

In this cleaning work, instead of saying Indu assisted Vani, it might be better to say that Vani assisted Indu. Most of the work was done by Indu. It was Indu who thought of where to keep each thing; how to arrange things so that they would look beautiful and found places for everything. Helping Indu carry heavy things she couldn't manage on her own, bringing her things she asked for, that was what Vani did. By the time they finished, the house had acquired a new charm. Vani was extremely surprised and happy that her house looked so different now.

Vani was by nature lazy. It was her tendency to think that any job could be done tomorrow. Saying tomorrow, tomorrow, all her work would remain pending for the morrow. That was why, naturally, her house had never looked as beautiful as it did that day.

That evening Ratna came home early. He was also very surprised to see his house in such order. Before he even finished drinking coffee, he got to know that Indu, from the neighbouring house, was the one responsible for the new look of the house. When he got to know this, he felt, "If only my Vani would also take greater interest in household chores." In five years of married life, he had realized that fulfilling his desires was not as easy as he had hoped. But still, he had not been disappointed to such an extent that he no longer harboured any hope of things changing. Once in a while he would think, "Wish it was this way…wish it was that way."

When Ratna returned from work, usually tired, Vani would be in Indu's house, chatting. After Ratna came, she would run back home and make coffee for him. Before Vani's coffee was ready, someone or the other would have come to call Ratna. Several times, he would have to leave without eating or drinking anything. Then for some time, it was true that Vani would feel bad, "Aiyo, I should have prepared coffee and food quickly," but that was only for a while.

The next day, the same thing as usual…it was also like that with Ratna's clothes—though he had enough clothes, it was difficult to find even one tie when he needed it.

When they first got married, in the blush of new love, Ratna had not noticed any of these things, but as days went by, he would think, "Why is my Vani like this?" But when he saw her repenting face and eyes full of tears, he wouldn't know what to say and he would console her, laugh and make her laugh. All his attempts to be a little angry, to tell her not to do this again and to teach her a lesson would end this way.

As the days went by and their friendship grew, Indu began to notice Vani's negligence. Even if she did not know, when something like this happened, Vani herself would tell Indu. She would curse her idiocy. Initially, Indu would console Vani. But after understanding it was in her nature, she was surprised and would think, "Even though she has got a husband like Ratna, she cannot keep him happy, this Vani. If he was my husband, how I would behave," one deep sigh. Then, "Thoo, mad thoughts," and a clouded smile.

3.

One morning at around eleven o'clock, while Indu was cooking, Vani came home. There were no time restrictions for Vani coming to Indu's house. From the time she woke up in the morning till she went to bed, running from this house to that house, that house to this was her habit. There was nothing special in her comings and goings. But Vani's visit that day was the cause for much turbulence in Indu's peaceful life. Vani did not come for any particular reason. She had kept lentils to cook for the saaru and, thinking she would have to sit idle until it cooked, came to Indu's house to chat.

Having a lot of work in the afternoon, Ratna came home early that day to have lunch quickly and go back. Vani was not at home. He called a few times. There was no reply. Finally, when he came to the backyard to see if she was there, he heard her voice from inside Indu's house. He got a little angry thinking she was passing time in the neighbour's house instead of finishing chores in the afternoon. "Vaniiiiiii," he called a little louder.

Amidst the excitement of talking, she did not hear him, and in all that noise, neither did Indu. Immersed as they were in talking, when Ratna came near the backyard fence and again called "Vaniiiii", they got a bit frightened.

Vani said, "Aiyo, Indu, I haven't finished cooking still," and hurried outside.

When Indu followed her and came near the door, she saw Ratna near the fence looking tired. Vani was asking, "How long have you been back? Do you have to go to the hospital right away?"

Listening to her, Indu thought that Ratna was going to starve today too. Even though Ratna might have had this experience several times before, it was the first time Indu was seeing it herself. She felt very bad thinking that she had also helped Vani waste time gossiping. As she looked at the tired and harried Ratna through a crack in the door, these thoughts began to form in her heart. Thoughts that had never before occurred to her began to come one after the other. As if to follow them, a long, deep sigh escaped her. She wiped her tears with the end of her saree and went inside. By then Vani and Ratna had reached the jagali of their house.

4.

Indu went inside. Just a moment ago, there was peace, joy and some kind of satisfaction in her life. Then there was pride in her house, its beauty and cleanliness. For some reason, the joy, pride, peace, satisfaction, all that she had just a minute ago, seemed to have vanished. Instead, their place was taken by difficult questions that came and engulfed her. "Vani, who doesn't know the value of anything, why did god give Vani everything but made my life full of darkness?" seemed to her like the biggest question of all. No matter how much she thought about it, she could not get answers. Lost, she sat where she was till evening when Vani came again. The food she had cooked remained untouched.

Indu used to earlier feel compassion when she saw Vani's gloomy face, but that day her weepy face made Indu feel a little happy. 'Should god reserve all sorrow for me alone? Let Vani also get a small taste of it," she told herself. Even though she knew thinking like that was selfish of her and that Vani was not responsible for her sorrows, Vani's wilted face did not arouse any sympathy in her.

When Vani cried and said, "He never says anything, today he got angry and just walked away," Indu felt a kind of joy.

But the very next instant, she thought that it was wrong to think like that. When her heart reminded her that she had never before given space for such feelings, she felt ashamed of her own meanness. To repent for such thoughts, she consoled Vani and helped her with her chores.

After Indu finished all the work, she returned home just as Ratna came back from work. He had not been at peace since that afternoon. He had never been angry with Vani before. The dis-content he had suppressed for many days had that day, propelled by hunger, turned into anger. When his anger began to dissipate, he was a little ashamed of his behaviour. Wondering how sad Vani must be feeling, he came straight home without even going to the club. Vani was not lying on the bed crying, neither had she ne-glected to light the evening lamp, like he had anticipated. Thanks to Indu's handiwork, the house was looking new and shone with light. Vani was waiting for him with a smiling face and food already prepared.

But his surprise and joy at seeing all this lasted only one second. He did not fail to notice when he began to eat that the food Vani was serving was the handiwork of the neighbour, Indu. Instead of thinking, "If only my Vani was also skilled like this….," like before, he began to wonder what Indu might look like; he had never seen her before. All the things Vani was saying to please him felt like they were coming from a distance. Seeing him distracted, Vani thought to herself, "He is tired from being hungry all day," and vowed, "this should never ever happen again in the future."

She had made these vows several times before, but none of them were ever kept. This time, because Indu was helping her with work all the time, Vani did not find adhering to her promise too difficult. To tell the truth, it was Indu who was fulfilling Vani's vow.

5.

From the day Indu began to spend most of her time helping Vani with chores so as to not give space to wayward thoughts, their household began to run smoothly. Ratna did not fail to notice these changes at home. The more he saw all this, the more his appreciation for Indu's skills grew, though he had not yet seen her. He would think of Indu while seeing every orderly and maintained thing in the house. Even if he had not seen her in person, he imagined a picture of her. His imaginary Indu was a model woman. Along with all the qualities needed to be a perfect housewife, she was also immensely beautiful. But for some reason, there was no smile on the face and no laughter in the eyes he had imagined. Maybe that was because he was used to looking at Vani who was always smiling and laughing. Since she was in every way different from Vani, he must have imagined Indu as not having a smile on her face.

As time went by, imagining her had become a hobby for Ratna. Once in a while, thoughts of Indu would come to him even when he was in the middle of a lot of work. These thoughts caught him by surprise. What madness was this! He would get a little angry too. But like Vani's promises, it was all for a little while only. For Ratna, who could cure impossible diseases with the strength of his medicines, it felt like he could not escape the disease of drawing Indu's picture in his mind. The only solution he could finally think of to completely erase the imaginary picture was to see her in person. He thought that she was not going to be as beautiful as he had imagined, and seeing this in person would make his obsession fade away.

It was not difficult for Ratna to see Indu. He knew that she came to his house whenever he was not there. If he came home unexpectedly, he knew she would be there. One day, saying that he would be home late that evening, he went out, but came back home before it struck three o'clock. Just as he had expected, he could tell Indu was inside from the conversation he could hear. He went in slowly.

There was Indu, ironing and folding his clothes from a bundle that was on the table in the living room, standing with her back to the door. Vani was sitting on one corner of the table, her legs extended in front of her, lost in the excitement of the conversation.

Ratna stood near the door for five–six minutes, but neither of them noticed he had come. Ratna saw his wife, unleashing a rain of chatter, and he saw Indu, lost in work but still giving Vani appropriate answers where required. Seeing the stark contrast between the two of them, he began to draw a new picture of Indu, even though he had come with the intention of completely erasing her from his mind. Yes, even though the real Indu did not have the exceptional beauty of the imaginary one, her diligence filled that difference. Five, ten, fifteen minutes passed, but Ratna did not move from where he stood. Then Vani, for some reason, turned towards the door and seeing Ratna, said, "How come you are so early? To go to the cinema, is it?" she asked, and got down from the table.

Only then did Indu realise that Ratna had come home. Thrown off balance by his unexpected return, she quickly kept the iron down and turned. The parts of her face that had been incomplete in Ratna's imagination were now complete.

When Indu turned, she saw Ratna looking at her without blinking and left the work she was doing, and walked back to her house through the back door. Thinking that Ratna had come home early to take her to the cinema, Vani, in her excitement to ask him questions, did not stop her.

About an hour and a half later when Vani went to Indu's house to take her along with them to the cinema, Indu was sleeping and said she had a headache. Vani's efforts to persuade her failed. It was true that she had a headache—but what Vani did not know was that the reason for it was a problem that could not be solved. If she knew, she wouldn't have brought Ratna to Indu's house.

Ratna had gotten ready to go to the cinema in the hope that watching a film would help erase Indu's image from his mind. But ever playful, Vani had said, "Let's also take Indu," and even as he was resisting, she ran to go call Indu.

When Vani returned, he was a little relieved to see that Indu was not with her. But when she said, "Check on Indu and give her some medicine," he got a little angry at her silliness.

"What is the big deal about a little headache? Give her one aspirin tablet and come soon, we will get late!" he said, a bit rudely.

If it was any other time, he wouldn't have minded examining Indu and giving her medicine. She would have joined the list of patients he saw day and night.

But just then, when he was trying to forget Indu, Vani forcing him to go to her house seemed vulgar. How could Vani's simple nature realize this? She would not relent, however, and finally dragged Ratna to Indu's house.

Ratna had never thought that he would see Indu again the same day, just a few hours apart, that too in her own house, as a patient. He could not have dreamed that the next time he saw her, he would find her crying. Yes, Indu was crying…like a small child, she was sobbing in little gasps. Even though she knew she was not sobbing because of the headache, she did not know exactly why she was crying either; the reason was that delicate.

She had started crying after Vani left, knowing there was no one around. How would she know that Vani would bring Ratna to her house?

The only reason Ratna and Vani could think of for her crying was her extraordinary headache. Indu stopped crying when she saw them. She was very embarrassed that they had seen her crying, and because Vani had brought Ratna without warning. Ratna felt the same too. Indu…seeing the crying Indu, all other thoughts vanished from his heart, and he felt like consoling her in the way small children are consoled. But what stopped him was Vani standing close by and several years of experience seeing patients. Though there was a war of thoughts in his head, he put on a serious face and touched her forehead. He turned towards Vani and said, "There is fever too."

In reply, Vani said, "You give her some medicine and go to the cinema, I'll stay here," and ignoring Indu's protests sat down right there.

Ratna went to the cinema alone. But that night if Vani had asked, "What film did you watch?", he would have had to reply, "Indu's crying face."

6.

That day's headache became the foundation of Ratna's and Indu's acquaintance. Where earlier Indu used to feel shy around Ratna, now she talked to him without any inhibitions. Going with them to the cinema was also included in her list of things to do. This way, within six months of the house next door being rented out, Indu's solitary life changed completely. It changed, that was all....

It would be wrong to say that she got much peace or happiness from it. When she first came to that house, the pride and satisfaction she had had in the thought of her house, herself, her happiness in her independence, these were no longer there. Having previously thought that she was happy and could remain so, after seeing Ratna and Indu's family life, she realized that there was a void in her life. Though initially the feeling was vague and unclear, it began to take form the longer she was in their company. Maybe it was also because Ratna was always thinking about her too! Her heart had begun to lean towards Ratna, despite her best efforts to stop it.

While such thoughts were taking birth and slowly growing in the hearts of Indu and Ratna without each other's knowledge, Vani had to go to her mother's house suddenly. It had been decided that both husband and wife would go for a month in summer after Ratna got leave. But since her mother had unexpectedly fallen sick, her brother came to take her first. It had not been possible for Ratna to get leave then. That was why Vani went back with only her brother.

Before she left, she told Indu, "Indu, Amma is sick; I will come back the moment she is well. Until I come, take care of my house too a little."

Ratna was also standing there. Unable to say anything else, Indu said, "Hmmm."

Telling Vani "hmm" was all she could do, because after she left, Indu did not go near her house. She was by nature scared of any wrongdoing. She had grown up thinking that society's rules and norms were god's rules. When she realized that she was attracted to Ratna, she had been very scared. After Vani left, her fear grew tenfold. How did I give space in my heart to such thoughts? Why? Such questions began to bother her constantly. But along with these thoughts, Ratna's image had also taken form in her heart. Even though she knew that it was inappropriate to love Vani's husband, she could not do anything about it. Fearing that Ratna might get to know of her inappropriate love for him, she did not go near his house at all after Vani left. She stopped caring for the flowers and plants in the backyard as well, fearing she might see Ratna.

Now there was only one medium to help Indu kill time: weaving day dreams in a world of imagination, and bringing herself to tears thinking of how they were just dreams after all.

Ratna who saw Indu every day when Vani was there, now felt very sad that neither of them was around. It was only when Indu stopped coming around that he realized how she had invaded his heart little by little when she used to visit their house every day. So even though he thought it was best that she didn't come, his fickle heart was impatient for one glimpse of her.

After Vani left, he ate his meals at the hotel and lived in the club. He came home only to change clothes and to sleep at night. He used to stay in the club until the last person left. Then after having dinner in the hotel, it would be past eleven o'clock by the time he reached home. Still, if he came home in the daytime, he would go to the backyard and see if by any chance Indu was there.

Though it had been two months since Vani had gone, there was no indication that she was going to come back any time soon. One day when Indu was drawing water from the well, Ratna came near the fence in the backyard. After Vani left, that was the first time they had seen each other. While they used to talk uninhibitedly when Vani was there, they found nothing to say just then. Fearing that her feelings might be exposed if she remained silent, Indu asked, "When is Vani coming?"

Instead of replying to her question, Ratna asked, "Are you well, Indira? What is this, I don't see you at all these days?"

That was the first time she had heard her name from his lips. Till that day, she had never realized her name was so beautiful.

The way her name changed just because it was uttered from Ratna's mouth made her smile. Her eyes, revealing all the secrets of her heart, looked at his face. Ratna's eyes also did not keep his feelings hidden. It was that look of his that brought Indu back to earth from where she was, high, very high in the air, and made her aware of her duty. The very next instant, without even taking the pot of water she had drawn from the well, she went inside. Though Ratna stood there for a long time, she did not come out again.

The next day, the day after, the day after that, Ratna waited for Indu for three days, but he did not get even a glimpse of her. The fourth day, Indu got a letter in the post. Familiar with Ratna's handwriting, she knew it was his, the moment she saw it. Instead of opening the letter, she held it in her hands and sat thinking. It remained unopened when she got up after a very long time; it was wet though with her tears. She got up and carried the letter to the kitchen. In another minute, it turned to ashes on the stove.

* * *

After another week, Vani came back from her mother's house. She went directly to Indu's house. The house was locked. Vani's surprise knew no bounds! With no one to call her own, Vani wondered where Indu might have gone. She inquired in the house opposite hers. She was told that Indu had gone to the house of the people who had raised her. Upon hearing this, she was all the more surprised. Indu had always said that she would never go to those people's house. Why she had chosen to go there was something beyond Vani's understanding. She never got to know the reason for Indu's strange behaviour. Since Ratna, who knew, did not attempt to tell her, this matter remained for ever an unsolved puzzle for Vani.

Atonement

1.

During the Dasara vacation, Murthy came back to the village from Bangalore. He was the only son of wealthy parents; his mother's beloved doll. Even though he was twenty-three years old, his mother still pampered him like he was a two-year-old. No matter what he did, his mother did not think it was wrong. She followed rituals of purity very strictly, and they were more important to her than her life, but still, one day when Murthy entered the kitchen wearing shoes, she forgave him saying, "Poor thing, he is a little boy, what will he know." Murthy too loved her more than life itself. He never went against her wishes. If he got even two days off in college, he would run to the village to see his mother. His mother was like a brother, sister, friend and everyone else to him. Murthy loved listening to her sweet words of love. Those who saw them together said they were like friends instead of calling them mother and son.

Murthy's father was a man of very strange character. His heart was as hard as Murthy's was soft. He liked accumulating money and loathed spending it. When he saw Murthy's suits and shoes, he would grumble that it was all a way to waste money. His habit was to beat his wife whenever he was angry with his son. Unable to bear the cruel punishment meted out to his mother, Murthy stopped asking his father for money. On the first of every month, his father would write a letter, one and half foolscap sheet long, about how "spending money is a sin" and send him fifteen rupees with which Murthy had to manage for the month. On the thirtieth of the month, Murthy had to send an account of every paise spent to his father. If the way he had spent the money seemed fair, his father would send him money the next day. This apart, his father wished for Murthy to come first in every class every year. The previous year Murthy had come second in class, and his father had not talked to him for a month. Blaming his mother's excessive love and friendship for this, he had given Murthy's mother several beatings as well.

Unable to see his mother's agony, Murthy was determined to somehow come first in class this year and studied day and night. Mother and son's love grew stronger day by day because of the father's cruelty.

The day Murthy came to the village, his father had to go to Bangalore for some work. That day, his mother finished all household chores quickly and sat talking to her son on the jagali at the front of the house. Little girls from the neighbouring houses, wearing nice sarees, were running here and there on the road in excitement, curious to see the Navarathri dolls displayed in various homes. Seeing those little ones happy and dancing, mother and son stopped talking and became silent. Murthy's mother loved children. One of the children running around on the road (about four years old) was very cute. Her family had draped a small saree on the child. It seemed like it was the first time she had worn a saree. Her joy knew no bounds. Her curly hair was flying in the breeze, her vast eyes like black bees in the middle of long lashes, red lips on her mouth were spilling with laughter. Singing some song, the child tucked a doll under her arm and was happily walking along the road when Murthy's mother said, "Come here, Prabha."

Hearing her call, Prabha came running and showing off her doll said, "Aunty, look at my doll."

Murthy's mother lifted up the bundle of cuteness, and kissing her cheeks said, "Look Murthy has come, talk to him," and went inside to bring them snacks to eat.

"Look at my doll, Murthy," Prabha began talking to Murthy.

Murthy had known Prabha for many years. She was their neighbour Narayana Rao's daughter. When Nalini carried little Prabha and stood near the fence in the backyard talking to his mother, he had taken Prabha and played with her several times. When two old friends meet, is there an end to their conversation? By the time Prabha went to her house that day, it had gone past eight. Murthy dropped her back home.

2.

The next morning, Murthy climbed the champaka tree in the backyard to get some flowers for his mother. The tree was very tall. While he was plucking some flowers from a high branch, he saw their neighbour Nalini sitting by the tap, scrubbing utensils. On the jagali, adorable Prabha was feeding a young calf some roti with her little hands. Prabha's beautiful face, lit by the rays of the tender sun, looked like a lotus bud that was about to bloom. Her playful eyes beamed swirls of happy smiles. Her hair had not been brushed yet. Her tousled hair framed her face and it looked like the tendrils were kissing her. Murthy looked at her and forgot the world. That was how beautiful and innocent the child looked. Prabha had not seen Murthy. Once the roti was finished, she went in to get another. Then Murthy woke up from his reverie, "Prabha is so cute! I wish I had a sister like her," he thought, and letting out a sigh, he continued to pluck the flowers.

A little later Murthy turned to see if Prabha had come out. She had not. Nalini was still sitting and scrubbing vessels. He could not see her face. Murthy could see only her long braid that was swinging about on her back. Murthy was familiar with that braid. That was how he knew that it was Nalini who was sitting by the water tap.

Nalini was Prabha's aunt's—her mother's elder sister—daughter. She was from the same village. With her father and mother no more, she was an orphan. Her father had passed away the year she was born. Two years later, her mother had died by suicide. From that day on, Prabha's parents had become Nalini's parents too. Her aunt was looking after her older sister's orphan very well.

People told the story of Nalini's mother's suicide in many ways. Nalini's heart ached from listening to people talk about her dead mother. Though her uncle had tried very hard to get her married, people commented, "Her mother was not of good character and morals. The daughter will also have taken to the mother's ways," and though she was fifteen years old, no one had come to marry her.

Murthy knew her from childhood. "What is the daughter's crime if the mother is not of good character?" he would ask.

When Murthy was young, he used to play with Nalini. He used to pluck flowers for her from the tree. He used to draw pictures for her. As they grew older, they stopped talking. Murthy went to Bangalore. The other reason was that Murthy's father had ordered him not to talk to Nalini. Though Murthy was not afraid of his father's command, he kept quiet fearing his mother would get into trouble. It had been four–five years since he had spoken with Nalini. It had not been difficult for him to stop talking to her. After going to Bangalore, he had even forgotten that a person called Nalini lived in the world. Now when he saw her braid, he remembered the little Nalini of the old days. He remembered her love for flowers. Thinking there was no harm in giving her a few flowers, he broke off a small branch that was full of flowers and threw it near where she sat. Hearing it fall, she turned and Murthy saw her face. Instead of the face of the Nalini who used to climb trees, break fences, throw stones and run around with him in those days, he saw a face that was trying very hard to hide some kind of intolerable agony that she could not mask; seeing this the soft-natured Murthy said "Aiyo" to himself. Nalini saw the flowers that had fallen but did not see Murthy on the tree. Thinking that they must have fallen in the wind, she washed her hands and took the flowers.

On taking the flowers in her hands, a faint smile formed on her face for a moment, like the sun peeping through the clouds for just a minute, and then disappearing. Thinking that her smile was a bigger reward than what he had hoped for, Murthy climbed down from the tree without being seen and went inside looking for his mother.

3.

There was no doubt that Prabha was beautiful. Her face was like the lotus that awaited the sunrise to bloom. Nalini was not beautiful like Prabha but when a rare smile dawned upon her sorrowful face, it looked like a fully bloomed lotus. Prabha was of rosy-white complexion. Nalini had blackish-red skin. Prabha's eyes were playful. Nalini's were still and serious. When those eyes were looking at something, an indescribable grace played on her face: the way a startled doe might look at a bright light.

For three days, Murthy climbed the tree and without her knowing, watched Nalini wash vessels. He gave Prabha snacks, brought her home and sent her back with flowers, asking her to give them to her mother. He knew the flowers would reach Nalini as well. The young, mischievous Nalini had never imposed any power on him, but now the beauty of her serious eyes began to make an impression on Murthy's heart.

Murthy's mother greatly loved the orphaned Nalini. When her husband was not home, she would call her and Prabha home, braid their hair and give them snacks to eat. She had shed tears several times for the sorrows in Nalini's life without anyone's knowledge. "Oh god, make Nalini the wife of a good man and may she remain happy," she would pray in her heart every time she saw Nalini.

It had been six days since Murthy had come home. That evening his mother was sitting on the jagali at the back of the house and was doing Nalini's hair. Murthy had climbed the tree and was plucking flowers for Nalini. Prabha was standing under the tree with her little hands outstretched, begging for flowers. Murthy threw a flower for her from above. Holding it, Prabha asked, "For Nalini?"

"If she asks, I'll give," said Murthy. Though Murthy had been looking at her for the last six days, it was only that day that Nalini had seen him. It had been four–five years since she had talked to him. Murthy who used to play with her earlier was now in college, studying for his BA.

Nalini became very shy when she heard what Murthy said. Though she loved flowers, "I cannot ask Murthy," she thought to herself.

His mother asked, "Why, Nalini? Can't you ask him for a flower? Why are you hesitant with Murthy?"

Her head already bent from shyness because of what Murthy had said, she buried her head further down and asked, "Murthy, a flower for me." She had asked for one flower! But Murthy came down from the tree and brought a basket full of flowers, which he poured over her head. Until then she had been staring at the ground; now with a tiny smile of gratitude, Nalini's eyes looked up at Murthy's face for a brief second and disappeared behind her lashes.

Murthy's mother said, "See, with your mischief, you have now ruined the hair I had done up," and laughed.

Little Prabha started arguing, "I got only one flower, Nalini got many."

Murthy did not hear anyone's words. The brief glance Nalini had given him with that faint smile was dancing before his eyes.

4.

Murthy's holidays were over. He had to leave the next morning by the eight o'clock bus. All the preparations for his departure were done. Seeing Nalini was the only thing left to do. But how to see her? The bus would leave before she came to wash the vessels.

Going to their house just to see her was impossible. Using Prabha as an excuse was also ruled out because she was already in his house since morning. Sighing loudly because it would not be possible to see Nalini, he boarded the bus that had come by the front of the house after paying respects to his parents. Though she was sad that he was leaving, his mother smiled, looked at his face and in her heart, prayed, "God, it is your job to protect my son."

Two weeks after reaching Bangalore, Murthy wrote a letter to his mother about Nalini. Indicating that he wished to marry Nalini, he begged his mother to write to him about her. Though his mother was happy at the thought of her son being married, also at the prospect of Nalini becoming her daughter-in-law, she knew that her husband would not approve, because of which she was more sad than happy upon reading Murthy's letter.

Though Nalini had committed no crime, Murthy's father had strong reasons for rejecting her. People did not know, but he knew in his heart that he was the reason her mother had died by suicide. Neither Murthy nor his mother knew this. But they both knew that he would oppose Nalini becoming his daughter-in-law. While writing to her son, Murthy's mother would write about Nalini. Her joy would know no bounds if Nalini became her daughter-in-law, she thought. But when she thought of her husband, her joy would turn into sorrow.

The days went by one after the other. Murthy did not allow for disappointment and began to study with joy and enthusiasm; so that after passing his exams, he could get a job, liberate his mother from the cruelty of his father and then marry Nalini.

Finally, the day of his exams arrived. Having studied well, Murthy did not find them tough and wrote them well. The moment his exams were over and holidays began, he left for the village. This time, not just with the usual enthusiasm of seeing his mother, but also with eagerness to see Nalini.

His father was a little relieved that Murthy had done well in his exams. In his glowering eyes, when he saw Murthy, a whirl of love would twirl and disappear like the sun coming out during the monsoons. His anger towards Murthy's mother also reduced. Seeing his father calm and at peace, Murthy waited for a chance to speak to him about Nalini.

Four days had passed since Murthy had come home. That afternoon, after lunch, he was returning from the bathroom after washing his hands. He had to cross the front yard to get to the bathroom. When he came to the yard, Prabha was standing near the fence and called out, "Murthyyy."

Murthy went over and lifted Prabha up and over the fence. She had finished lunch too but had not yet washed her hands. "Nalini will come to wash my hands. I will hide here. Don't say anything," she said and sat down.

When he heard Nalini's name, Murthy stood there. After four–five minutes—it felt like four–five hours to Murthy—Nalini came carrying water in a small pot and called out Prabha's name. Prabha did not answer. She slowly retreated and ran into Murthy's house. Not finding Prabha, Nalini approached the fence where Murthy was waiting. She saw him and blushed. She began to turn back.

Murthy asked, "Nalini, why are you running? Am I a tiger?"

"I have to wash Prabha's hands. She is hiding somewhere," she said and took a step forward.

"Prabha is in our house. Wait a minute, Nalini," said Murthy earnestly.

Nalini turned back and asked, "Do you need me for something?"

"What is this, Nalini, so shy with me? Don't you know me? Have you forgotten how you used to fight with me?" Murthy asked.

"We were small children then; why bring up those things now?" Nalini replied and started to turn away.

"Hold on, Nalini, you are in such a hurry! You were small then. Have you grown so big now that you can't say two words to an old friend?" he asked.

"Not that, Murthy, I did not say that."

"Then what is it, Nalini?"

From inside, her aunt called, "Naliniiii- Naliniiii- Naliniiiii."

"Aunty is calling, I have work, I have to go." Nalini ran away before Murthy could say another word.

When Nalini disappeared, Murthy's face became like the moon covered by clouds.

Aunty is calling! I have work! I have to go!

Nalini, my Nalini has to run when others call! Even though his heart was impatient, he knew he did not have the right to keep her beside him.

Deciding that he had to talk to his father to be able to make things right, he went inside. His mother was having lunch. Prabha was sitting next to her and talking. Instead of sitting with his mother to chat, he went to the living room where his father was reading the newspaper. Seeing his son, he kept the newspaper down on the table and looked at Murthy's face in surprise. It was not common for Murthy to go looking for his father. This was the first time Murthy had approached his father with such courage. Upon hearing what he had to say, Murthy's father sat like a statue in astonishment. Finally, after properly understanding what he had meant, in a harsh tone, his father replied with only one word: "No."

Murthy had expected this answer. So, he was not shocked. With conviction and courage, he said, "I am going to marry her. Forgive me for going against your wishes."

5.

Murthy stood first in the university. Not just that, he got the job of a private tutor at a wealthy zamindar's house. Thanks to the recommendation of his professors and his own capabilities, his salary was not low either. A long-desired wish was fulfilled and Murthy became independent. All that was left now was to bring his mother to live with him and then to marry Nalini.

But then, no one gets to fulfil all their desires. That year, in a critical condition after a deadly fever, his mother lay her head on her son's thigh, blessed him, saying, "Marry Nalini and live happily, my darling," and made her journey to the afterlife.

Murthy's tower of dreams lay broken. His life's guiding star had disappeared. His mother, who had been part of all his joys and sorrows, excitement and happiness, who used to shower him with love, was now no more. For Murthy, who thought life was full of joy and happiness, it now seemed without essence.

His father had stopped talking to him from the day he got to know of Murthy's feelings for Nalini. Who was left now? Nalini Nalini Nalini! It was impossible to live without her.

After one year, against his father's wishes, Murthy married Nalini. The minute the wedding rituals were over, Murthy held her hands, looked into her eyes, smiled and asked, "Nalini, my Nalini, from now on, you won't have to run saying 'Someone is calling, I have work, I have to go.' I now have the right to talk to you for however long I want."

Shedding tears of happiness, Nalini replied softly, "My lord, it is all your mercy."

That night, reading the letter seeking forgiveness that Nalini had insisted Murthy write, his father sighed thinking, "This is the atonement for my sin." When he woke up from the bed the next morning, his pillow was wet with tears of repentance.

Sanyasi Ratna

1.

Raja and Ratna were friends; they studied in the same class. They lived in the same hostel. They were the same age; from the same community. Raja was the only son of his parents. Ratna had a younger sister. Except for this, they were exactly the same.

Raja's marriage was fixed with Ratna's sister. From childhood, Raja had liked Ratna's younger sister Seetha. Her parents had agreed to give their daughter to Raja and Seetha had also said yes. Since there were no other obstacles, it was agreed that they would get married right after Raja finished his BA.

Ratna did not agree on this one thing—not that his sister shouldn't marry Raja—but that just like him, Raja should not get married at all, he thought; he would get angry if the issue of marriage was brought up. He would place his hands over his ears and say, "Thoo." Any time the topic came up, Ratna would say, "I will become a sanyasi. I will always remain a bachelor. Don't talk to me about marriage." Raja and Ratna would debate this issue every day.

One night, after they were talking about this and that, Raja asked, "Lo, Ratna, did your sister's letter come?"

"What is this madness? Her letter came just the other day. I haven't even replied to that...will she write again before I can write back?" he asked and started laughing.

"Why are you laughing?" Raja asked.

"Seeing your madness."

"Wait, one day you will also go mad."

"There is no chance of such madness in this lifetime."

"We will wait and see."

"What is there to wait and see? You see it right now…I am a sanyasi."

"Ravana was a sanyasi…."

"Shut up…don't talk too much…I will get angry…"

"Do sanyasis get angry then?"

"Look…don't start your goading. Believe me…I will definitely not get married."

"You will certainly get married."

"I don't have the desire to fall into the pit of samsara like you."

"You will fall into a bigger pit than me, wait and see. Then I will tell you that I told you so."

"Okay…when that happens you tell me….now shut up and sleep."

"I will sleep….but if you get married, tell me what you will give me."

"Give? What give? If I get married only then the question will arise."

"Let's say you do get married. What will you give then?"

"If I don't get married, what will you give me, tell me that first."

"The camera that I bought the other day, I'll give you that. Now tell me what you will give."

"Me….I will give you the ring on my finger."

"Is that true?"

"Yes, true. At least now go to sleep."

"Hold on, I'll sleep…but…"

"Now what is this 'but' about…?"

"Nothing. In two years you will be married."

"You will have to give up your camera…you are going to lose it."

"It looks like your ring loves my finger…before the end of two years, the sanyasi's true face will be seen."

"Shut up and sleep."

"Time for the ring to come to me," Raja said, as he switched off the lights and went to sleep.

"He is mad," Ratna said and shut his eyes. But both of them did not fall asleep for a long time that night.

2.

The year Raja finished his BA, his grandmother died. That was why his wedding was postponed that year. Grandmother was old, she died. But Raja was sad that he had to wait another year to marry Seetha. That same year, he had to leave for Madras to study law. Raja did not have the heart to leave town without making Seetha his own. Couldn't grandmother have died after the wedding, he thought. Under the pretext of talking to Ratna, not a day went by without Raja going to their house to see Seetha at least ten times. Ratna used to be very amused seeing Raja's behaviour. Every time Ratna laughed, Raja would say, "There is a time for the mother-in-law and there is a time for the daughter-in-law," implying that he would soon get a chance to make fun of Ratna for the same reason that he was being teased now.

Ratna would retort, "Let me know when it is the daughter-in-law's time."

"It will certainly come, let's see how it won't come," Raja would look at the ring on Ratna's finger and reply, laughing.

The holidays ended. They left for Madras together. While leaving Seetha, Raja was unbearably sad; Ratna could not control his laughter looking at Raja's state. Finally, the train started and eventually, they reached Madras.

One evening Raja and Ratna were walking near the beach. That same day, Ratna had received a letter from Seetha. Whenever her letter arrived, Ratna's habit was to give it to Raja after reading it. That day, he hadn't given Raja the letter to tease him. Raja was eager to know what was written in the letter; he feared that Ratna would tease him if he asked for the letter. Ratna was stubborn that he would not give the letter until Raja asked for it. Finally, Ratna's stubbornness won. Raja asked, "Ratna, did you get a letter from home?"

"Yes," Ratna replied

"What news?" Raja asked.

"Nothing much."

Raja wanted to ask about Seetha; but if he asked, it would be paving the way for mockery. Finally, desire trumped his ego.

"How is your sister?"

"She is the way she is."

Raja was not satisfied with this answer. "Give it, let me see," he said.

"It is a letter written to me, why should I give it to you?" Ratna said.

"Just give it…don't tease me."

"Say please and I will give it."

Though Raja's ego stopped him for a while, again it was his desire that won. "Please…now give it to me," he said.

"God knows what is in this piece of paper to beg so much," Ratna laughed and gave him the letter.

"Your time will also come, then you see what I'll do," Raja said and sat on a bench to read the letter.

Ratna walked towards a friend who was coming that way and began talking. After chatting about this and that, the friend said, "A Miss Vani has come from the Mysore region. She is singing. Come, let's go."

Ratna greatly loved music. "Raja, are you coming," he asked.

If he didn't read Seetha's letter at least a hundred times, Raja wouldn't be satisfied. "I am not coming, you go," he said.

Ratna went to Miss Vani's music concert with his friend. Raja remained on the bench committing Seetha's letter to memory.

3.

It was ten o'clock at night. Raja was sitting in his room with Seetha's photo in front of him, reading her letter for the hundred and first time. Ratna had still not come back from Miss Vani's concert. He finally returned at ten-thirty. Raja was still meditating on Seetha.

Instead of teasing him as usual, Ratna quietly came and sat on a chair. The moment he saw Ratna, Raja hid Seetha's photo and got up. Raja had not noticed the time pass. He saw the clock and asked, "Where were you out so late, Ratna?"

"Have you forgotten already? I was at Miss Vani's concert. It ended just now…I came straight here."

"How was the music?" asked Raja.

"It was Vani who sang," replied Ratna.

"Is she from Mysore?"

"Yes. She is still a young girl, can't be more than eighteen years old. In both beauty and raga, she is Vani itself, a beautiful angel," Ratna said.

"What is this, sanyasi? You have started describing beauty and raga!"

"Do you think a sanyasi had no eyes? If I say it like it is, what has it got to do with sanyasa?" asked Ratna, a little annoyed.

"Now you say no…but what if the sanyasi goes mad over music and beauty?"

"The monkey got destroyed, and now wants to destroy the whole forest. You know that proverb…if I give my ears to your words…. Like you said, what will happen if…this is all you will talk about. Come let's go for dinner."

The next evening after coming back from college, Raja changed his clothes and sat down to read a novel. Ratna was wearing a new suit and standing in front of the mirror combing his hair. "Raja, aren't you coming for a walk?" he asked.

"I am not getting up until I finish this novel, you go if you want," Raja said.

Ratna did not force him. He checked his face in the mirror once more and went out. That day by the time Ratna came back, it had struck nine o'clock. Raja had been immersed in reading his novel and hadn't noticed how late it was. The next day too, it was ten o'clock by the time Ratna came back from his walk. Raja hadn't gone out with Ratna because he had to write a letter home. Though it was time for dinner, he decided to wait for Ratna so they could eat together. Ratna did not return for a long time and Raja got tired of waiting. The moment Ratna came…

"Where were you for so long? I got tired of waiting."

"I was talking to Narayana and did not realize how late it was."

"Come, at least now let's go to dinner. What were you both doing for this long?"

"Some chatter…come let's go eat."

After coming back from dinner, Ratna said, "Lo, tomorrow there is Vani's concert, at three o'clock in the afternoon. Will you come?"

Raja exclaimed, "College!"

"Let's just take French leave…she sings very well. If you listen to music, you should listen to Vani." Ratna insisted.

"What is this! Have you agreed to advertise Vani's music? You are always ready to praise Vani," asked Raja.

"Listen to her sing once. Then you will surely say that she is really an angel," Ratna said.

"Okay, I will come and see your Vani tomorrow then," Raja agreed.

4.

"How was the music?" asked Ratna.

"It was okay…she sings well…but…" Raja said, cautiously.

"But what?"

"Her singing is not as great as you described. Listening to you, I wondered how good she must be, but now…"

"Now?"

"She is like us; nothing extraordinary," Raja said. "Aiyo dim-wit, her singing before you is like playing a flute before a buffalo, both cannot appreciate the music. Look at her beauty and tell me how good her voice is."

The music ended before Raja finished talking. People began to leave. Ratna said, "Wait a bit, Raja, I'll come in a minute," and went away.

Though he had said he would come in a bit, Ratna did not return for one hour. Raja got fed up and went and stood outside. By then, Ratna came back, talking to two people and went to a car that was parked there. The people who came with him sat in the car and drove away. Ratna stood with his hat in his hands, watching till the car was out of sight. Raja walked up behind Ratna, placed a hand on his shoulder and asked, "Who were they?"

Ratna got a fright and gasped, "Who…?"

"That is what I am asking, who were they?" Raja asked.

"Oh them—you don't know them."

"How will I know if you say that? If you say it was Miss Vani and her father, I will get to know well," Raja said, controlling his laughter.

Ratna did not reply.

"How did you get to know them?"

"Narayana and Miss Vani's father know each other. He introduced me the other day."

"Oh, so that was why it took the sanyasi that long to come back that night? It must be a characteristic of sanyasa, of renunciation to hide things like this…isn't it?"

Ratna did not answer. Raja burst out laughing and said, "It has come…the time has come for your ring to come to me."

Then too Ratna did not speak. On the way back, "Raja, you won't get the ring," Ratna said.

"Why is that?"

"Will Vani marry people like us? You'll only get the ring if I marry, isn't it?"

"This level of sanyasa has arrived? If she marries you, learn how to put tala. Then it will be all right."

"Lo, don't joke. I am really serious about this matter."

"I am sorry. But will your parents agree?"

"Convincing them is my job, but Vani has to agree first."

"Aiyo, sanyasi, has the time come for you to fall into the pit of samsara? I want to cry looking at your state."

"Just shut your mouth."

"This is the daughter-in-law's time…the mother-in-law's time has passed…"

5.

"Raja…"

Raja, who was reading, lifted his head and asked, "What is it, Ratna?"

"Come here."

"You are writing something. Should I help?"

"That's why I am calling, come." Ratna replied impatiently

"Aiyo, sanyasi, have you become used to writing love letters also now?"

"Make fun after you help me. Look at this, is this enough?"

After reading, Raja could not control his laughter.

"What is this, Ratna. It looks like you have written this after watching a movie. Vani will die laughing when she reads it."

"Then how do you write? You are experienced, can't you tell me?" Ratna begged.

"Why did my madness get to this sanyasi too?" Raja wondered and wrote a letter for Ratna. They posted the letter.

A reply came from Vani the very next day. Reading Vani's acceptance, Ratna began dancing. Raja laughed and said, "So this is the sanyasi's true face," and began to dance with him.

There was no trouble like Raja and Ratna had anticipated; Ratna's parents gave their approval. Glad that the sanyasi had finally agreed to be a householder, they got Ratna and Vani married that very year. On the day of the wedding, the diamond ring on Ratna's finger was transferred to Raja's finger. "The sanyasi has got salvation," Raja said.

The next year, Seetha became Raja's. Now, Raja and Ratna were similar in every aspect. Whenever he got an opportunity, Raja would tease Ratna. If he was told to be quiet, "This is the daughter-in-law's time, the mother-in-law's time has passed," Raja would reply and shut Ratna up.

The Wooden Doll

1.

Two months had passed since I joined school. Our house was in the village so I had to stay in boarding school. Since I was a village girl, I did not know the ways and manners of the town people. All my classmates would do their hair nicely and wear nice clothes. It was not that I didn't have nice clothes; but they were all old fashioned. I did not know how to do my hair. That was why all the girls would tease me, calling me "village girl" and "goggu" disparagingly. No one made friends with me.

Since English was not used much in the village school, I did not know how to answer if I was asked a question in English in class. If the teacher scolded me and asked why I didn't answer her question, I would start crying. Seeing my tears all the girls would burst out laughing. Their laughter would drown me in shame. After I left my village, I was not happy even one day. I was sad for not being able to see my mother, the girls' mockery, and then there was also punishment for not knowing English. The enthusiasm I had when I left home had vanished. I used to wonder why my father couldn't come and get me. The Mother Superior would read all the letters I wrote. Given all this, I used to think it was better to say goodbye to the school and go away. I decided that the next time Anna came to meet me, I would go back with him.

One day I did not go to English class saying I had a headache and was sitting in my room. I was very upset by the behaviour of the other girls. Since there was no one there, I sat crying by myself. I heard the door open. Though I had closed the door, I hadn't latched it. I turned. It was Shyla; she and I were classmates. Though she lagged behind in studies, she always came first in sports and in making mischief. Though the girls made fun of her in class, once out of class, they were all scared of her. Seeing her there, I wiped my tears. She came in and sat down on my bed. Though it had been two months since I had joined the school, she had never spoken to me. That was why I was surprised when she came to my room. She got to know I had been crying when she saw my face. "Why are you crying, Seetha?" she asked; I did not reply.

She got up, placed her hands on my shoulders and asked again, "Won't you tell me why you are crying?"

I began to sob even more. She very tenderly held my hand and said, "Is it anything you cannot tell your friend? If you need any help, tell me."

Seeing her friendliness, my sorrow increased. Finally, I calmed down and told her all that I was feeling.

"Do you have to cry for such things? I will make all your sorrows go away. So what if you don't know English? Have I learnt anything much? Even now I came because I was sent out of class for not studying. I peeped in because I heard you crying. Is it a big deal to work a little harder and learn your lessons? From today you and I are friends. From now on, if anyone says anything to you, tell me," she said.

I held her hands in gratitude. I could not speak. By then the bell rang for the second period. Both of us went to Kannada class.

2.

Shyla had studied in that school from kindergarten. Everyone was her friend. The girls did what she told them to. Even if she put pins on the chair that the teacher sat on in front of everyone, no one said that it was Shyla who did it. She made up nicknames for every teacher. If she decided to, she could have stood first in the class. She was not dumb. She could solve in just one minute a math problem that none of us could understand. But more than studies, her heart was in play. To do what she had been told not to was her greatest desire. She would do anything for her friends. That was why all the girls loved her. She loved me like a sister. I was not sad like earlier, but after becoming Shyla's friend, the other girls treated me with love too. I worked hard and gained a better understanding of English. Being in school began to feel good.

One day when the teacher went out, we all started talking instead of studying. On hearing the noise we were making, the teacher came back and said we had to stay without food that day. We stayed hungry till the evening. After that we couldn't bear it. But what could we do? Since we had broken the rules of the school, we had to stay hungry and repent. We were not allowed into the mess hall that day. Seeing our weepy faces because we couldn't stay hungry any longer made Shyla very sad. She was the one who had started making noise that day. The thought that all the girls had to stay hungry because of her made her weep. Seeing her sob, we all began to console her. But she would not feel better until our stomachs were full. It was decided that somehow our hunger had to be satiated.

Shyla asked, "Do you all have money?"

We had money.

But "Can we eat money?" Vinoda asked.

"Money cannot be eaten, but with money one can buy things to eat," Shyla replied.

By then, it was nine o'clock at night. It was a distance of half a mile from the school to town. Who would bring something to eat from there? All the security guards had gone to sleep. Even if they had been awake, it was against the rules to bring food for those who were being punished.

Shyla said, "I'll go to town and get something to eat."

We refused to send our Shyla to town at night. We did not have permission to go outside the school compound even in the daytime. Then how would Shyla go out alone at night? They had locked all of us who were starving in the hall. How could we unlock the door and get out? But Shyla did not think it was difficult. She said she would jump out of the window. The window was twelve feet above the ground. It was not easy to jump. Shyla said she would jump and show us.

"If we are going, let us both go," I said.

"You are all starving because of me. I will go alone," she said.

Finally, it was her stubbornness that won. She tied my saree to the grills of the window and used it to get down. "Bear your hunger for half an hour. By then I will bring the food," she said and disappeared into the night.

3.

The clock struck nine-thirty; Shyla did not come. Ten o'clock; no sign of Shyla. It struck ten-thirty; no sound of Shyla. The moment she went, we had thought, "It is okay if we are hungry, we should not have let her go."

We got very scared when we did not see her coming. Why hadn't she come yet? What had happened to her? We had let her go out alone; we began to berate ourselves. It was okay if we did not have food. It was okay if we were hungry. We began to pray for Shyla to return. As though god had heard our prayers, Shyla climbed in through the window and stood before us. Her clothes were dirty. Her hair was in disarray. Her face was sweating. But her eyes were laughing. Seeing her smiling face, our worries vanished.

"Why did it take so long, Shyla?" I asked.

She replied, "First, eat. Then I will tell you the story." We all hurriedly ate the food she had got.

After eating she said: "I went to town, got the food and had almost reached the school. Two drunkards were fighting and coming in my direction. Before I could find a place to hide, they saw me. There was no one else there. Thinking I was a ghost, they started chasing me. I began to run. By the time I was nearing the town,

I saw someone coming towards us. I stood still. Seeing me stop, the drunkards also stopped.

"The man approaching us asked, 'Who are you, girl? Where are you going at night?'

"I did not say anything. I pointed towards the drunkards. The drunk men saw the man and ran away. I did not say anything else and started towards the school again. The man asked, 'Where are you going alone at night?'

"I did not have time to think of a lie. I told him the truth.

"Then he asked, 'What is your name?' I told him.

"'It is wrong of you to have come out at night like a tomboy. If the drunk men had troubled you, what would you have done? I know your father. I shall walk you till the school. Let's go,' he said.

"I got angry with him for calling me a tomboy. But since he knew my father, I didn't want this man to tell him about this incident, so I stayed quiet. When we got near the school gate, I requested him, 'Do not tell my father about this.'

"'I will think about it,' he said and went away. I came here. This is my story."

Then Vinoda asked, "How did your saree get dirty?"

"I fell down while running," Shyla said.

Hearing of all the trouble Shyla had gone through for us, our love for her increased.

"Who was the one who rescued you from the drunk men?" I asked.

Shyla said, "I don't know him." Vinoda wanted to know,

"How was he to look at? Was he an old man or young?" It looked like the question made Shyla a little angry.

"How could I see what he looked like in the dark? Old, young, I don't know," she said.

Still, Vinoda asked, "What was his voice like? Won't you recognize him if you see him again?"

Seeing Vinoda's curiosity, Shyla's anger turned to amusement. "I could recognize his voice. But how can I tell you what his voice sounded like? It was soft, I can say," she said.

"You must marry the hero who rescued you from the drunk men. Now that is romance," Vinoda teased.

"Find him. I will marry him," replied Shyla.

All of us burst out laughing. Since our stomachs were finally full, we began to feel sleepy. We slept on the benches.

4.

We had a teacher who taught us mathematics and Kannada. Since he had retired, another teacher had been appointed. He had not yet taken charge, so we had not seen him. The previous teacher was an old man, and Shyla had named him Ajjayya, grandfather. We had a meeting to decide what to name the new teacher. Shyla was its president. A lot of nicknames were suggested. None of them sounded right. It was not possible to name him without seeing him. The president concluded the meeting with a speech saying that the right name could be decided based on his personality and after seeing if he was good, bad, old or young. By then it was time for class.

It was time for mathematics. Since there was no teacher, we were happy that we did not have to do maths. Shyla did not want to sit still. She wanted to do some mischief. She asked all of us what we could do, but we could not think of anything. Finally, she herself thought of something fun. Her habit was to do something as soon as she thought of it. She went to the dressing room, brought Sister Margaret's cap, and wearing it on her head, sat on the teacher's chair. We couldn't control our laughter when we saw her in that long cap, contorting her face to look like Sister Margaret.

She said, "I am the new teacher. You must all listen to what I say. Now write an essay about the time Sister was sleeping in class and the Reverend Mother came and woke her up."

We all started writing hurriedly to get her approval. We finished writing too. We went up to Shyla one by one to show her. We got titles like good, fair, etc., depending on the essay. She read all our essays. Only mine was left, and I went up to show her. "This is very good, the whole class should copy this," she said and began to read it loudly.

"Sitting on the chair and snoring, our Sister...," she did not finish the sentence. Reverend Mother had come into the class with someone new. The girls who were standing around talking quickly went back and sat down in their seats. I was standing near the table. I could not go back to my place. Shyla was sitting on the chair.

Mother thought she was Sister and said, "Sister, he is..." By then she realized the one she was addressing was not Sister. She came closer. She saw Shyla and started to laugh; but she pretended to be angry and said, "What is this, Shyla?"

She replied, "Since the teacher was not there, I was teaching the girls."

She asked, "What is it that you are reading?"

"The essay that Seetha wrote," replied Shyla.

Mother did not know how to read Kannada. She took the book, gave it to the new person and said, "Read what she has written, see how it is."

He began to read it quietly. We began to get scared of the consequences. Only on Shyla's face, a small smile began to dance. After reading, he looked at Shyla and said, "It is very good."

We were all surprised hearing his words. Wondering how Shyla felt, I looked at her face. I was even more surprised. Shyla never let anyone see her feelings. But that day, her face was like a mirror to her inner feelings. Both her eyes reflected surprise. If she was that surprised, we knew there had to be a very strong reason. I kept quiet thinking I'd ask her that night.

Mother was happy to hear that what Shyla had asked us to write was good. Poor thing! What did she know, that Sister's madness was what was reflected in those essays! If she had known, Shyla would have had to stay hungry that day. Instead, she patted Shyla's back and said, "You should not touch other people's things. Go put the cap back."

After Shyla returned the cap and came back to her seat, Mother introduced us to the new person. He was our new teacher Krishnamurthy. By this time, since the period was over, the new teacher did not make us do maths. We came out of the class talking about him. That night, I asked Shyla the reason for her surprise. "Just like you all, I was also surprised to listen to what he said. What other reason could there be?" she said.

To see her keep something hidden when she never used to lie to me only made me more curious. I forced her to tell me. At last she said, "The man I saw on the road that night is him. Don't tell anyone this."

I promised her that I wouldn't.

5.

Our new teacher's name was Krishnamurthy. He had earned a BA degree just that year. Though he wanted to study law, because of financial constraints, he couldn't go to Madras. It had been decided that he would teach in our school for one year and then go to Madras the following year. Our classmate Shankuntala's house was next to his house. She knew him from childhood. She was the one who told us all about him.

Krishnamurthy used to come to teach us five hours of maths and three hours of Kannada every week. The moment he came, he would write one or two math sums on the blackboard and explain how to solve them. While solving the sums, he would explain to us while looking at the blackboard, without turning to the class to even ask if we understood or not. Then he would write similar sums on the board and tell us to solve them. When we were working on the sums, he would sit in the chair with his face bent. Sometimes he would be looking at some book. Not even once would he look towards us. Every day, this was the same routine.

In Kannada class, he wouldn't look at our faces while asking us questions. When he asked, those who knew would answer; he wouldn't even call upon anyone to answer. One day, he asked a question about something. Like Shyla had instructed us, even though we knew it, none of us gave him the answer. Then he said, "Among so many people, none of you know the answer? What a shame!"

Then Shyla stood up and asked, "Who said we don't know?"

He asked, "What is the meaning of not answering?"

"We must not answer without being asked to, Reverend Mother has told us," Shyla said.

He got angry at Shyla. "Can't any one of you hear? I asked you a question just now," Krishnamurthy said.

Shyla replied, "Yes, it is true that you asked a question. But who did you ask? We all know the answer to it; should we all stand up and answer?"

Krishnamurthy's face turned black with anger. "Can't one of you answer?" he asked.

"We all have names. Does one of us mean the wall?" Shyla replied.

"Then you only tell the answer...blabber mouth!" he said.

"My name is Shyla," Shyla said and answered the question.

That evening when we all gathered around, we praised Shyla for getting Krishnamurthy, who never talked to anyone in class, to open his mouth. Shyla, the president of that day's meeting, gave him the name "Wooden Doll".

Since he used to act like a Wooden Doll in class, we all approved the name. "Who will teach the wooden doll the ways of a human?" Shakuntala asked, jokingly.

"That job belongs to Shyla," said Vinoda.

Shyla said, "It is best if Shakuntala takes up this job. More than us, she is better acquainted with Wooden Doll. Their houses are also close to each other."

Shakuntala said, "So what if our houses are nearby? While coming out, if he sees me, he turns his face and goes. Even if I know him from childhood, he is shy to even look in my direction. Is it then possible for me to teach him to be civilized?"

It was like a discussion in a meeting of mice about who would tie a bell around the cat's neck. Who in our group would teach Wooden Doll the business of being a human being? A long debate ensued. It was not easy for anyone but the wife he would marry to do this; but for someone who wouldn't even look in the direction of women, would he get married? It was decided that somehow, he had to be married so that his wife could teach him a lesson. But who would get married to him? We elected the intelligent Shyla among us to marry him.

I said, "Shyla, this is the right time to take revenge on him for calling you a tomboy and a blabber mouth. Do not lose this opportunity," and laughed.

From my words, all the girls got to know that Wooden Doll was the one who called Shyla a tomboy the other day. Vinoda started clapping her hands and danced, chanting, "romance, romance." Shyla laughed at Vinoda's joke, got up from there and left. That day's meeting was over.

6.

Though she agreed to marry Wooden Doll, even smart Shyla did not think it was easy to accomplish this. After the day Shyla provoked him in class, he started writing the questions on the board and would ask us to write the answers in our notebooks. After we wrote them, he would read and give us marks depending on the writing. Though we called him Wooden Doll behind his back, once he came to class, even Shyla couldn't go against his words. One day, by the time we finished writing answers for some questions he had written, the period was over. He said he would read our answers and give our notebooks the next day and took them with him. The next day we all got our notebooks.

When we were all writing in class, Wooden Doll used to look at one book. Its cover was green. It used to be in his pocket all the time. Though he had been coming to our school for six months, he still hadn't finished reading that book. He used to look at that book all the time. What was in that book that he is so faithfully reading it? Shyla was very curious. She was eager to somehow take a look at that book at least once. How to see the book that was always in his hands? But once Shyla had stubbornly made up her mind, was it difficult? She made a plan.

We were all doing maths. He was, like always, reading the green book. Shyla quietly got up from her place, took the maths books and approached him. Since none of us ever went to his seat, he was surprised to see Shyla there. He kept the book he was reading on the table and looked at her face in surprise. Shyla kept her book on the table and said, "I don't understand this maths sum."

"Which one?" he asked and took the book in his hands. When he was looking at her book, Shyla took his book from the table and looked at it. I was watching her face. Her face had turned red. She kept the book back on the table. Wooden Doll saw this, quickly kept the book in his pocket and looked at Shyla. Wooden Doll's face turned redder than Shyla's. The very next instant he bent his head down and showed Shyla the method to do the sum. After the sum was done, Shyla came and sat down in her seat.

After the period was over, I asked Shyla what was in the book. "It was a Hindi book. I don't know what was in it," she said. Though I knew she was lying, I did not force her to tell the truth. I guessed the truth.

The next day, Shyla did not come to maths class saying she had a headache. As usual, Wooden Doll came to class with his head bent. He wrote the sums on the blackboard. Before he sat on his chair and started reading the green book, he turned towards the class. I saw from his face that he noticed Shyla's absence. That day, Wooden Doll's eyes did not have the same enthusiasm while looking at the green book. His glance would frequently fall on Shyla's seat. Seeing his every action, I thought that he was sad about something that day. To find out why, I asked Shakuntala, "Did something special happen in his house?"

"A little while before coming to school I spoke to his elder sister. If there was anything special, she would have told me," Shakuntala said.

Then it struck my dim brain. The reason for Wooden Doll's sadness was that Shyla's seat was empty. That afternoon we had Kannada class, and Shyla's headache was gone. She had gone and sat in the class before the bell rang. When we all went in, she was in her seat reading something. Though it looked like she was reading, she was not. When I went near her, she was holding the book upside down and laughing. I did not understand the reason for Shyla's laughter. Before I could ask, Wooden Doll came in. The moment he came in, Krishnamurthy's eyes went to Shyla's seat. When he saw Shyla, he began to look at the floor.

Later, he wrote questions on the board and went to sit in his chair. We began to write answers to his questions. I hadn't even finished one sentence, when there was a loud thud of something falling. We all lifted our heads in alarm.

Wooden Doll was holding the chair off which he had fallen and getting up. His face had turned red from the embarrassment of having fallen in front of all of us. With embarrassment also came anger. "Who kept the areca nut under the chair?" he asked us, angrily.

Since none of us had done it, we kept quiet. I realized why Shyla had come to class before the bell had rung. Seeing us all quiet, he said, "Until you tell the truth, none of you can leave the class."

Then Shyla got up and said, "I kept the areca nut."

"After the class is over, write 'what I did was wrong' a thousand times and go," Wooden Doll said and sat down.

The period ended. We all came out. Shyla was alone in class. Wooden Doll sat guard in his chair to see that she did not go out.

We all drank coffee. Shyla still had not come. I went to see what Shyla was doing through the window. Shyla was sitting in her place and writing. Wooden Doll was walking from one end of the class to the other. After a while, Shyla said, "I have finished writing," and stood up.

Wooden Doll went near her, read what she had written and asked, "What is this that you have written?"

"Can't you read?" asked Shyla.

"You have written that it is difficult to teach Wooden Doll human behaviour. What does that mean?" he asked angrily.

Shyla replied, "That means that it is not easy to get married to Wooden Doll."

"Why should anyone marry a wooden doll?" he asked.

"To teach it human behaviour," Shyla said.

Then he asked, "Who is the wooden doll that does not know human behaviour? Who is the one marrying it?"

Shyla said, "Wooden Doll is the one who keeps someone's photo without asking and looks at it. The one who will marry him and teach him human behaviour is me."

I did not stand there to see what happened next. We all gathered under the jamun tree and waited for her. After half an hour, Shyla came to where we were sitting. Shyla was not that good looking; but her face was shining with a unique glow like never before, one that made us want to keep looking at her. A smile had overflowed from her eyes, spread open her lips to show two rows of pearl-like teeth. Some tendrils of her curly hair were kissing her red cheeks. "I finished writing, I got the job too," said Shyla.

As if I didn't know, I asked, "Which job?"

"To teach Wooden Doll how to be like a human," she said.

We were all happy that, as usual, Shyla had managed to fulfil the task she had undertaken. We all began to discuss what to give her as a present for her wedding. But unlike the previous time, Shyla was not the leader at this meeting.

* * *

The other day I had gone to Shyla's house with my son Vasantha. Wooden Doll was now a prestigious criminal lawyer. When we went, Shyla and Krishnamurthy's three-year-old son Prabhat was standing on the jagali of the house. Seeing me, he said, "Amma, Aunty has come," and ran inside.

Shyla came out carrying him. We sat under the grape vines in their front yard and talked. Vasantha and Prabhat were playing in the yard. When Krishnamurthy came back from the court at five o'clock, we were still there, talking. The children were also playing nearby. Seeing him come, Shyla went inside saying that she will get coffee.

When Krishnamurthy came in to the room, I was sitting alone. Seeing me, he asked, "When did you come, Seetha? Are you well?" Lifting Vasantha up, he asked, "What is your name?"

"Vasantha, the name Shyla suggested," I said.

It was half an hour by the time Shyla brought coffee. Till then Krishnamurthy was chatting with me. While drinking the coffee, I looked at Shyla who was sitting near me, and laughed.

"Why are you laughing?" she asked.

"Shyla, you are really smart. You have taught Wooden Doll really well. The Wooden Doll who used to bend his head down if he saw us, now has been speaking with me without hesitation for half an hour," I replied and laughed.

"After marrying a tomboy and a blabber mouth, if he does not follow her wishes, will it do?" said Shyla and looked at Krishnamurthy with love in her eyes.

"Yes, Seetha, this tomboy gives me a lot of trouble. Give her some advice," Krishnamurthy said, and gave Shyla a light punch on her back.

"Look at Anna hitting me," Shyla complained to Prabhat.

"Don't hit Amma," Prabhat told Krishnamurthy, gave his father a small punch and sat on his mother's lap.

Seeing how our childish pranks had turned into this loving family made my eyes shed tears of happiness.

A Small Picture

1.

8.4.24

Raghu,

Why is it that you have not written at all since you left? Waiting for your letters has become a job for me. You seem to have forgotten all the things you told me when you were here. Raghu, from the day I stepped on a sinful path with you, I have not had peace in my heart. Even if I am yours in front of god, if people come to know, they will scorn me. You told me that you would make me yours by marrying me in front of society. It has been two months since you left and there is no news from you. Why is that? Don't you want me anymore? I do not know much. You are the one who pushed me into the muck; if you don't lift me out from there, who will? I beg you, don't leave me, Raghu.

Yesterday, our maid's daughter, who had run away with someone a few years ago, came back. When she left, she was a girl of seventeen. When I see her now, it seems like she must have been pretty then. The man whom she ran away with has left her now. Do you know what athige, sister-in-law, said when she saw her? "This is the right punishment for you." From then on, my heart keeps saying: get ready for punishment.

Raghu, is there no punishment for the one who ruined her? There cannot be, because he is a man. The crime is always the woman's. The man who took her down the path of sin must by now be trying to do the same with another woman. But there is no punishment for him because he is a man. Morality puts pressure only on weak women.

Raghu, don't get angry that I wrote all this. When I think of her, I begin to think of all kinds of things.

I beg you not to make me suffer the way she is suffering. Even if you cannot love me like you did that day, at least give me a little space in a corner of your heart. Do not reject me....

Yours,
Shantha

2.

10.4.24

Shantha,

I received your letter. I was surprised to read it. You have written that I was the one who pushed you into muck. I pushed you because you were so eager to fall in. If you were such a saint, you should have had some sense earlier. What is the use of blaming me now? All is fair in love and war.

If there is anyone else who wants to marry you, go ahead. I do not have any objections.

Raghu

3.

5.5.24

Raja,

Not a single reply to my previous letters. Why? Are you in any trouble? Can't you tell me what is worrying you? If I can do something, do not hesitate to ask; I will help as much as I can.

Hoping that you will at least reply to this letter....

Yours,
Nana

4.

7.5.24

Nana,

I received all your letters, but forgive me for not replying to any. I sat down to write to you several times, I wrote many letters. But I did not have the courage to drop even one in the post box. I am in great difficulty. Why should I make you a part of my troubles? There is nothing you can do. Why should I subject you to grief by telling you my problems? Do not be angry that I did not write; forgive me.

Yours,
Raja

5.

12.5.24

Raja,

Why do you have inhibitions with me? I used to be part of your happiness. Why are you denying me a part in your days of grief? What has happened to your friendship? You used to share everything with me, so why are you trying to hide things now? Even if I cannot do anything, I will still be there for you. If you truly consider me a friend, write to me about what is troubling you. Just like I was a partner in your happiness, I will be there for your problems also, remember that….

Always yours,
Nana

6.

Nana,

There is nothing that I cannot tell you. Even if I don't tell you, this is something you will get to know anyway, so what is the use of hiding it?

You have met my younger sister Shantha. When you saw her, she was a little girl of ten. By then she had been widowed, you know that. When Amma was dying, she said, "Raja, Shantha is an innocent child, protect her." Nana, I did not fulfil Amma's last wish. Damn my sinful life!

My wife was not treating Shantha well. I did not know this earlier. Now I know. Aiyo…

Six months ago, my wife's older brother had come. Even though I knew he was not a good man, I had felt that he would not do anything bad to me. If I or my wife had shown Shantha some compassion, she would not be on the streets today. Even though my wife saw Raghu (my wife's brother) take Shantha on a path to hell, she kept quiet. I, without knowing, and my wife, knowingly, together made Shantha's life hell. Right at that moment, Raghu came to hold her hand, seduce her with dubious words and take her away. Apparently, he had promised that he would join the Arya Samaj and marry her. After he left her and went away, it seems like those words also disappeared from his heart. About two months after he left, one morning Shantha was not to be found at home. She had left a letter on my table and gone away. The letter said this:

Anna, our family has never had a bad reputation, but I have brought disgrace to it now. Before others get to know everything, I am atoning for it. I did not have the courage to tell either you or athige about my condition. I do not have the strength to bear your grief or athige's contempt. Forgive me for leaving without telling you…Shanthu.

Nana, if I had treated her with love, she would not have become an outsider. I pushed Shantha away from our home. How can my heart be at peace? My life…

Forgive me…for telling you my problems and hurting you.

Raja

7.

20.5.24

Raja,

I received your letter just now. My heart hurt on reading it. Shantha, with her smiling face, who used to play with us in the old days is now…. Aiyo what is the use of us being there?

Raja, it is our duty to look for her. It is in our hands to find her and ensure that the rest of her days are happy. Get ready to go look for her instead of sitting idle in sorrow. I will come there by the next train to help. I feel that this is our duty.

Yours,
Nana

8.

21.5.24
Morning 12.30

Nana,

I received your letter, and along with it came yesterday's newspaper.

They say men are more courageous than women, that men can tolerate much more; I had thought that was true too. But after reading this newspaper, I could not bear it…I laid my head on the table. My wife is calling me for lunch. Lunch? Lunch for me who has killed Shantha?

Nana, why do you reminisce about old days? Those games, the happiness then, the joy…none of those remain. Isn't childhood man's happiest time? Mine and Shantha's childhood was too….

You must be wondering what was in the newspaper. "In a pond four miles from here, a woman's body has been found. She was pregnant. Her body has been kept at General Hospital. Her identity is not known. If anyone has information about her, we request that they come forward."

I went to General Hospital. Nana, I saw the dead body…it was Shantha!

A fair face. A kind nurse had put a red bottu on Shantha's white forehead…I cannot write anymore…

Raja

My Wedding

When I was a little boy, my neighbour's son went to England to sit for some exam and came back after touring Europe. Then, the respect the villagers gave him, his car, his new fashionable clothes, the way he walked, the way he spoke, all this made me long to go to England and come back like him. This desire took root in my childhood, and became stronger as I grew up, instead of being forgotten. It was because of this fierce longing to go to England that I did not fail even one year in school. I was the class topper; I was a model student in school. There was no one who did not hold me in high regard in school and at home.

After finishing high school and joining college, my desire to go to England became so strong as to trump every other desire.

My father had enough income to lead a comfortable life, but he could not afford to send me abroad. I did not know this then.

That year, I had sat for my BA exams. The holidays had started. The exam results had not yet come. I did not have any worries over the results though. I knew that I would pass in the first class.

During those holidays, my younger sister's husband Anantha, who was studying BL in Madras, had come home. The day he came, we were sitting around chatting after dinner when he said, "Ramu, after BA you will come to Madras, won't you?"

Before I could answer, father said, "After BA only BL is left, after all. The town is full of lawyers. But nothing else comes to mind. He will come with you. Ramu, what do you say? Will you do BL or an MA?" he asked.

Where is the dream of travelling Europe, ICS exam, car, etc.…. that I have dreamt from the time I could remember! And where is killing time as a lawyer after passing one's BL! I laughed.

"I wish to go to England, father," I said.

It is natural that every father wishes for his son to sit for a big exam, get a big job and earn a lot of money. But father did not have the means to send me to England. I realized that the moment I saw the slight hint of a smile on his face disappear.

"I wish to send you to England much more than you dream of it, Ramu. But tell me, what shall I do for the money?" he said.

Father's words let down the dream I had nurtured for many years and left me dejected. That night I couldn't sleep at all. Between the dream of many years and its fulfilment stood the obstacle of money. Money! Money! The whole night I remained chanting, "what will I do for money", "what will I do for money" without closing my eyes. I fell asleep at dawn. Even in my sleep, the same question of money, strange dreams.

When I woke up it was past nine. But I did not get up from the bed. Instead, I turned to the wall and kept thinking about money. I did not want to get up. I was lying in bed like that for at least another hour. Then, Ratna, my younger sister came and said, "Ramu, father is calling."

Hurriedly I got up, washed my face and went to father's room. There father and Anantha were talking. Seeing me standing by the door, father said, "Come here, Ramu."

I went inside and stood behind father's chair. Looking at my face, Anantha smiled and stood up. Father saw him stand up and said, "Don't go, Anantha," then turned to me and said, "You also sit near Anantha, Ramu."

From the smiles on their faces, I guessed that something was going on.

Once I sat down, father looked at my face and said, "Ramu, for a few days now I have been receiving several letters from parents saying that they will give their daughters in marriage to you. You are my only son. Your mother is also eager to see a daughter-in-law," and laughed softly.

It did not seem right to me that father was bringing up the topic of marriage on the day that my dreams were shattered. That apart, I had no interest in getting married for some time. In the realm of imagination, I had thought of the girl I would marry and had become jubilant. That was there, but why bring up marriage on the same day that my life's main goal was destroyed? I did not have the heart to hurt the feelings of father and mother who had never gone against my wishes. But still marriage! It did not seem proper to me to discuss marriage the day I had to let go of my dream of a grand future. But I did not have the courage to say so without hesitation.

Anantha was looking at me and smiling. Seeing me be quiet, father said, "Ramu, I did not want to get you married so soon either. But look, if you get married now, you can go to Europe like you wish. The girl's parents will finance your education. What do you say?"

I finally understood then why father had brought up the subject of marriage the same day that I had given up on my dream to go to England. I was a bit happy. But then, when there were debates in college, I had argued so many times that one should not take dowry. I had vowed that at my wedding, I wouldn't take one paise, and had thus shown off my machismo before friends who had taken dowry. I had strongly condemned this social evil so many times!

Now do I have to keep aside my dignity, go against my beliefs and go to England? Do I fulfil my lifelong dream or do I not betray my heart and keep my self-respect intact? Both are beloved to me. What shall I do?

Seeing me wordless, father said, "Think about it and tell me later," and went outside.

The moment father went out, Anantha began to lecture me non-stop. "What is it, Ramu? Why are you thinking? The offer came yesterday. Look now, if you get married, you can go to England this year itself. Till you come back, the girl will be in her father's house. She is now in her matriculate class. If you say yes, after matriculation they will send her to college too, it seems. She is learning music too. The girl's father is a zamindar, Ramu; she's the only daughter; taking money from poor people is one thing. When they are saying that they will give, why are you hesitating? You are a lucky chap, what do you say? Just say yes," he went on.

His words did not fail to interest me too. Yet, my heart did not agree to say yes immediately. "I will think and tell you by evening," I said.

"Do that," he said, patted my back and went out.

I sat alone in that room and began to think and rethink from all angles. Even by lunchtime I had not arrived at a decision. In the evening after a stroll, I was returning home when Anantha asked, "What have you decided, Ramu?"

I still hadn't decided anything. But accidently the word "okay" came out of my mouth.

"Congratulations, old chap!" he said and patted my back.

Aiyo, why did the word okay come out of my mouth. Having always trusted in love marriages, why have I sold myself for money? Is it marriage or is it trade…no, just for the sake of money why should I spoil a girl's life….?

But by then Anantha had gone in and told everyone that Ramu had agreed to the match. Everyone was very happy. Me? Even though I was about to succeed in attaining my life's main goal, I did not feel as happy as I should have felt.

The next day, Anantha asked me, "Don't you want to go see the girl?"

For someone marrying for money, what was the point in seeing the girl? "No, Anantha. I have said yes anyway, what is the need to see now?" I said.

He also said "your wish" and kept quiet.

It was decided that the wedding would take place at the end of the month. The girl's house was in Hyderabad. The wedding was to be in her house. Before the wedding, my exam results also came. I had been placed first in the university. My father and mother were happy; father and mother-in-law to-be were happy; Anantha and Ratna were happy; all my friends were happy. But the day I knew my dream would be fulfilled I was not happy.

From the day the wedding date was fixed, no one had time in my house. There was a conflict going on between the duality of wishes and disappointments at the same time in my heart. The days went by very fast and there was only one week to go before the wedding. The preparations for leaving for the wedding began. My uncles came with their wives and children from the village. Some people from the neighbouring houses also came. Finally, two days before the wedding, with great enthusiasm, everyone boarded the train. When we reached Hyderabad the next afternoon, they were waiting with cars to welcome us.

The house where we were dropped was huge. The girl's family lived in the house in front of this one. That house was also just as big, three storeys high. The girl's father, with a zari turban around his head, kept running from that house to this house and back, and made sure we were well looked after. He was father's classmate. But this was the first time I had met him.

A group of women from the opposite house came and peeped at me through the doors and windows just as we had sat down after lunch. Last year when father had bought a new motorcycle, I remembered how the neighbours had come to see it. I got up from there, pulled a shawl over my head and slept. But it kept bothering me that I had been sold.

* * *

The next morning at ten o'clock was the dhare, the auspicious hour of the wedding. Before that I wished to meet the girl who was to be my wife. But how would I see her? When I was asked earlier if I wanted to see her, I had said no. What would they think of me if I said I wanted to meet her now?

Still, at around four o'clock the previous evening I called Anantha and said, "Anantha, before getting married I want to see Shari once…"

Anantha said, "What is your hurry? You will see her tomorrow," laughed and silenced me.

* * *

At the mantapa, the wedding pavilion, Shari and I were standing opposite each other. Between us was a veil. Through the veil, I could vaguely see Shari. In just five more minutes I would see her directly before me! Still, I felt like those five minutes before the veil would be lifted were unending.

Finally, the veil was lifted. Shari was not like the queen from the world of my imagination; her skin was reddish-brown; she was thin and tall.

The priest said, "Place the garland, child."

She was looking straight at me and standing still. He said again "Place the garland, dear child." She was immovable.

Just then her mother came near her and said, "Shari, he is standing right in front of you dear, put the garland on him."

Her hands holding the flower garland came forward and I bent my head. She fumbled and slowly put the garland around my neck.

I saw her face again. The two drops of tears that had filled Shari's eyes fell on her cheeks and disappeared.

I understood then what no one who had come to the wedding from my side had realized.

My wife Shari was blind.

Sacrifice

1.

I had passed my MA exam. My parents were searching for a bride to get me married. Eventually, a girl was chosen. Her house was in a village twelve miles away from our house. Her parents were alive too. They were very poor, it seems. I had wanted to be the son-in-law of rich people. I badly wanted to go to England and become a barrister. I needed money if I wanted to go abroad. My father was not wealthy enough to spend too much money on me. If I had rich in-laws, I could have gone to England easily. That was why I did not have the heart to marry this girl from a poor family.

That evening, I had just returned from a stroll. My father was strict about following his rituals. Without fail, he used to do sandhya vandane every day. He wished for me to do all that too. While out, I had met some friends and, while talking with them, had not realized that it was time for the evening rituals. When I got back home, father was doing his japa chanting inside. I went into my room to change my clothes.

My sister Vijaya was sitting there, reading. I used to call her 'V.' Her habit was to sing devotional songs in the prayer room every evening. Seeing her sitting in my room, I asked her, "What are you reading, V?"

Throwing the book on the table, she replied, "I was not reading or anything. What is there in this book to read anyway."

"What is it, V? Aren't you going to sing?" I asked her.

"I finished already," she replied.

I was removing my coat and tie when she asked: "Anna, do you agree?"

"Agree to what?" I asked.

She replied, "As if you don't know anything! I asked if you agree to marry that girl."

I said, "I have not even seen her. What answer can I give?"

Then Vijaya said: "Anna, I have seen her. She is a good match for you in every way. She knows how to read and write. She is very beautiful."

I asked her, "How much dowry are they giving?"

Vijaya said, "Anna, father does not like taking dowry. They are very poor. But the girl is like the demi-goddess Rati. They had said they would give five hundred rupees. But father does not want to take that."

I said, "V, I want to go to England and study law. Only if they bear the expenses of that will I marry that girl. If not, I won't."

Vijaya asked, a little angrily: "Anna, you are an MA postgraduate. How can you say such things? Why do you want to sell yourself?"

I did not reply. She got angry and left.

2.

I finished my japa and came out of my room. My father also finished his japa and came outside. "What did you tell Vijaya?" he asked.

I did not say anything. "You will marry if they give you money for further studies, it seems. They are poor people. They have six or seven daughters. From where will they give money? You are not a small child who doesn't know anything. The girl is beautiful. I do not approve of you going to London by becoming the son-in-law of rich people. If you marry this girl, I will somehow give you the money you need to study law here. If you don't listen to me, you are not my son then. Think about it and tell me tomorrow," he said and went inside.

After a while, Amma called us for dinner. I said I was not the least bit hungry.

That night after everyone had slept, I went out. My mind was unsteady with anger. I had not the least desire to marry that girl. But I didn't have the courage to stand in front of father and say so. That was why I left the house that very night. The railway station was four miles from our village. It was midnight by the time I got there. There were still ten minutes before the train was to leave our village. I bought a ticket to Madras and went and sat in a compartment. There was no one else there. As I sat thinking what my fate thereafter would be, I fell asleep. I thought I heard a noise and woke up. I opened my eyes. The full moon was peeping in through the window. In the moonlight I saw someone sitting on the opposite bench. When we left my village, I was alone. Thinking that someone must have boarded the train along the way, I sat up. The man sitting in front of me was old, but he was dressed like a young man, so it was not easy to guess his age. It looked like he was wealthy from the kind of clothes he was wearing. The moment I felt he might be well-off, I wanted to make his acquaintance. Though he kept looking at me, it did not seem like he would talk. I had to start a conversation.

"Sir, could you please tell me what time it is?" I asked.

He looked at his wrist watch and said, "It is ten past two."

This old man was very talkative. After I spoke to him first, he continued the conversation. By the time we reached Madras, we had become friends.

The old man was a diamond merchant. When he asked who I was…I said I was from a poor family, that I had finished my MA and that I was going to Madras to look for a job. He told me to come meet him if I didn't find any work. By then we had reached Madras.

I went to the YMCA I had lived in when I was a student. Several of my friends who were studying law lived there. I stayed there that day, catching up with all of them.

I started looking for a job the next day. To my bad luck, I did not find a job anywhere. Two weeks had passed since I had come to Madras. The few rupees I had in hand were also spent. I could no longer afford a meal. Finding no other way, I went to the house of my friend from the train. By god's grace, he was at home when I went to meet him. He was very happy to see me. After talking for a while, he got to know that I had not found a job. He had a daughter and a distant niece. He asked me if I could take tuition classes for them. For someone who had found no other work, this felt like a big job. I agreed to tutor them.

I started classes the next day. His daughter was about fourteen, his niece about sixteen years old. His daughter was good looking, but his niece was gorgeous. It was the same with studies too. The daughter was average at her studies. The niece just needed to be told once and she learnt it. The daughter was very talkative while the niece would only answer if asked a question, and not say anything else. The daughter had a smiling face. The niece's beautiful face, though it looked burdened with some worry, there was a kind of…one could not get enough of looking…kind of beauty. The daughter's name was Seetha, Shanthi was the niece's name.

Six months had passed since I had started to take classes. Both the girls were advancing well. But Shanthi was faster at learning than Seetha. Shanthi's beauty, the sadness that seemed to envelop that beauty, her interest in studies, her restrained talking, all these had started pulling my heart towards her. No matter how much I saw her, I wanted to look at her more.

Though she was the daughter of a High Court judge's younger sister, her parents were not very well-off. They were trying very hard to fix her marriage. She was not yet married because they were too poor to afford a dowry. I was always thinking of Shanthi. If I married her, I could not go to London. That was why I tried to forget about her. No matter how hard I tried, her good qualities kept pulling my heart towards her. I could have married Seetha. Her father had called me son-in-law many times in jest. Seetha was his only daughter. He wanted to get me married to her and make me live there with them. I could have easily gone to London if I became his son-in-law. But from the day I fell in love with Shanthi, my heart kept telling me not to sacrifice love for the sake of money. But my desire to go to London had not reduced. That was why I was not yet ready to ask Shanthi's parents for her hand in marriage.

3.

It was nine o'clock. I was waiting for my students in the classroom. Truth be told, I was waiting for Shanthi. Just when I was thinking about her, I heard the sound of the door opening. Seetha came in through the door. There was no sign of Shanthi who always came with her. I felt sad not to see her. I hesitated to immediately ask 'Where is Shanthi?' But before I asked, she said, "Look, Sir, last night Shanthi's father came and took her away to their village. Do you know why? For her wedding!'"

That was when I realized that I couldn't live without Shanthi. I blamed myself for not having asked her parents earlier. What was the use now? After I had ruined my own life because of my greed for money I realized it was impossible for me to live in the world without Shanthi. I spent the day I lost Shanthi in distress. The next day during classes, Seetha showed me a letter. It was a letter from Shanthi that had come by that morning's post.

Dear Seetha,

I am causing you pain via this letter when you are happy; forgive me. I would not have written to you about my sorrow. But I don't have any other friend in this world apart from you. I have never done anything without telling you. Even now I won't do this thing I am doing without telling you.

Father has arranged my marriage. The groom is older than father. I am going to be his third wife. The groom has four grandchildren, it seems. The first groom who was arranged for me will not marry me because we cannot afford to give him a dowry. Seetha, I consider death better than spending my life like a corpse as that old man's third wife. Why shouldn't one do what is better? People say that suicide is a sin. If tying a small child in marriage to an old man is a virtue, then I prefer the sin of suicide to that virtue. By the time you receive this letter, your unfortunate sister would have left this world. I know at least you will not judge me as the sinner who died by suicide. Forgive me.

Yours,
Shanthi

I read Shanthi's letter. I cursed the man who demanded a dowry despite being given a golden doll like Shanthi. In my grief, I had forgotten that I too had once rejected a girl from a poor family. I blamed god. Instead of blaming god, if I had let go of my greed and married Shanthi, that sweet girl would have been happy. I berated myself for my mistake. God only knows how many young girls were sacrificed at the altar of the devil called dowry. I saw its true nature after it took the life of my Shanthi.

4.

I left for my village that same night. I reached home the next morning. When I reached I saw Amma had washed the front yard and was drawing a rangoli. My father and V were inside. When she saw me, Amma came and hugged me happily. I spoke to her for a while and went inside. My father was sitting in the drawing room. He did not speak even after seeing me. I did not stand there and went to my room. Vijaya was standing there looking at a picture. She saw me and hid the picture. In surprise, I asked her, "What are you looking at, V?"

She threw the paper she was looking at in front of me… "I was looking at the girl you murdered," she said.

I was very surprised. I looked at the paper hurriedly…

Shanthi's photo…but below it, 'Sacrifice for dowry'

Was Shanthi the girl I first refused to marry?

Now….what was the use!

Who is the sinner?

1.

Anna,

You must have received the last letter I wrote to you. You might even be surprised seeing this letter arrive before you have written a reply to me. I am writing to you because it is a matter of surprise.

You know Nagesh Rao who used to live near our house? Though you might be acquainted with him, you might not know everything about him. You might not have forgotten how, when we first moved to this house, we used to look at him and say "The eyes of Nagesh Rao are like the eyes of an evil man," and laugh. The silly thing we used to say as naughty children has now become true. He is more wretched than we ever guessed. You must be crinkling your eyebrows wondering why I am going on about his characteristics. Have some patience; I am writing this letter for Parvathy, who has fallen prey to his wretchedness and has been excommunicated from the community. Do you know who Parvathy is? She is the daughter of the Pandit who used to teach us Kannada. You know that the Pandit died the year he married Parvathy off. Last year, her husband accumulated a lot of debts and went her father's way. From that day, not knowing any other way to bring up her young child, Parvathy began to work as a cook in Nagesh Rao's house. This was all one year ago.

Parvathy tolerated Rao's abuse for the sake of her child. Along with the burden of his sins on her, he got her excommunicated and pushed her out of the house the other day. Last night, she was standing near the well with her child with the intention of dying by suicide, it seems. When Gaibi went to catch a cow that had escaped at night, she saw her and forcibly brought her here. If she hadn't forced Parvathy to come, today the corpses of both mother and child would have had to be removed from the well. I recognized her the moment I saw her.

When she saw me, the poor thing covered her face and started crying. She did not sleep all night. She fed the hungry child some milk. No matter how much we forced her, she herself did not touch anything. She has been fasting since yesterday. I am writing to you about all this because I need your help. She does not know where to go or what to do. Her community will not take her in. If we send her out from here, she will end up in the well. When we ask her what she will do she says, "I will stay here; at least for the sake of this child, give me shelter," and cries. That is why if you come here, you can properly take her into our community and pave the way for her future life.

Anna, you might remember that her father used to praise his caste. If the diktat of their religion is for a helpless orphan to do penance for the sins of an abuser, then no matter how much we thank god for not making us be born in that religion, it is not enough. If the Pandit was here to see all this, he would have had to change his opinions about his caste. Anyway; hoping that you will come as soon as you see this letter,

Your loving sister,
Unnisa

2.

Seethamma,

I have been thinking of writing you a letter for many days. I have just not found the time to write; did you at least find time now, you might ask. To tell you the truth, not even now. Kamala has fever; I haven't given her the medicine yet. I haven't bathed

Raghu yet. I haven't cooked also. But I have left all the work aside and sat down to write you a letter to tell you about something important.

You know Parvathy who used to dress up like a doll and go to school, that Pandit's daughter. Look at her, she has rejected her caste and joined the Muslim religion! When her father adored her too much and sent her to school, I knew she would turn out like this! This apart, look at this funny thing—Lakshmi from next door, she used to go to school with the shameless Parvathy, listen to what she says: "What will she do if not join that caste? Instead of trying to make sure she doesn't convert, you got her excommunicated, slammed the door in her face and showed her the way to the well to jump, so what do you care what happens to her?"

It was wrong to excommunicate her, it seems! I had to keep the fallen woman at home, it seems! Just look at the state of things!

It is late; I have to cook. I will write again when I am free.

Yours,

. . . .

3.

Nalini,

It has been many days since your letters came. Why are you not writing? Have you forgotten me once I was out of sight? It is natural; when you have many new friends, it is difficult to remember an old friend from the village. But no matter how much you try to forget me and even succeed, I will keep writing letters to you and remind you that I am also there in this world. For every ten letters of mine, if you don't write at least one letter, I will come there and make you use your precious time to talk with me. You will be scared of this threat, because when we were young, if I was being naughty, you and Parvathy would get scared and give me anything I wanted.

Do you remember, Nalini? Those games, jokes, fights, laughter, all that! We used to sit on the mound behind the school and picture our future lives. The memory of our happy daydreams. We used to think life was all about joy and happiness, Nalini! Now look how many of us have had to change our opinions. Look at our friend Seetha. Where are the things she used to wish for? The things she is suffering now! Did any of us ever think her fate would turn out like this? We used to tease Uma in class as mad, now she has become a big social reformer. When you see people craving to listen to her speeches, one begins to wonder "Is this that same Uma?" Shantha who used to say that she would never get married now has two children. Kamala who used to come first in class and was called intelligent, now has titles like stupid and bitch in her mother-in-law's house.

More than all this, there is another tragic news, Nalini, that too, about our dear Parvathy—how can I write about this, tell me?

Beauty, personality and behaviour, Parvathy had our appreciation in all this. You know that she became a widow and that she was working in Nagesh Rao's house. We hadn't imagined anybody else's life the way we had pictured hers, Nalini! "Our beauty will be the queen to a king and wear a crown," we used to say and rejoice. She has now been excommunicated from the caste, Nalini, because of Rao's sins. See, this is justice in our society! How many times we had argued with Unnisa saying that our caste, principles, society was superior! How many times we scorned Unnisa because she was a Muslim! Though the village is full of people from our caste, not one opened the door for Parvathy. There is place only for caste and not for compassion in the hearts of our people. All these caste rules are for women only. Men don't have to adhere to these rules. See, this is the mark of our caste's superiority.

When people of our great, very great caste showed Parvathy and her innocent child the way to the well, do you know who affectionately gave her shelter? Unnisa! Unnisa, who we used to call mleccha, laugh and show contempt for. Now tell me, Nalini, who is superior?

The whole town is condemning Parvathy for becoming a Muslim. They say that they knew she would become like this. All these educated people, why didn't they try to ensure that this didn't happen? I asked them. They said I was on Parvathy's side and now when I go to fetch water, the neighbours no longer talk to me.

Who is the sinner, Nalini? Who is responsible for Parvathy becoming Razia? Is it her? Or Rao? Or is it our cruel and rigid society?

What does it matter who it is? What has happened, has happened. She was not happy as Parvathy. I pray to god that as Razia her life is full of happiness.

Enough; I have nothing else to write.

Yours,
Lakshmi

4.

This was published in a local newspaper dated 8th:

It has caused the Hindus in the town much grief that the other day, a young Hindu woman has accepted the Muslim faith. To ensure that this does not happen again, a meeting of prominent Hindus took place under the leadership of Shri Nagesh Rao. It was unanimously decided in the meeting that the Hindu faith had to be protected.

...Who?

Mahesha,

"Are you married?" I asked you in the morning. It looked like my question took you by surprise. You said, "No." Your "no" took me by more of a surprise. Maybe you married that woman, I had thought.

During the last vacation, I invited you to our house. You gave an excuse saying you had to go to your village and did not come. But you did not go to your village. You were right here; that too with an immoral film actress.

Mahesha, I used to be proud of myself, thinking that I could get to know someone's personality just by looking at their face. That was why when I met you eight months ago, even though I did not know a single thing about you, I made you my bosom buddy. Your face inspired trust. I looked at your large, soulful eyes and thought, "Poor thing, he is a hurt soul; I should not hurt him by asking about the past." All the pride from that day has been reduced to powder now, Mahesha.

Though our friendship is just eight months old, you became more important to me than my own younger brother. I have never hidden anything from you. I believed that you had the same confidence and trust in me.

Why did you have to gain my friendship through deceit, Mahesha? Maybe you will ask, "My personal life is mine. What is the connection between that and our friendship?" In a way, there is no connection, it is true. You might find several friends who think like that. But after treating you like a member of our family in the *company of my mother, my sisters, this is not okay for me. One must be able to have love, respect, trust and honour in a friend. Until now, I looked at you with all those feelings. But after seeing you keeping company with a common film actress, roaming with her in broad daylight, how can those feelings remain? You noticed a change in my behaviour towards you and asked me the reason this morning. I could not look at your face and tell you why. That was why I had to write this letter.*

Mahesha, though I am from this town, I joined the hostel so that I could stay with you. We were both in the same room. Though it was just a feeling, I felt that you were an ideal friend. That every minute I spent with you was priceless. But it is impossible for me to stay like that now after the way you behaved. I am going to go back to my house today itself. Maybe we will see each other in college. Please do not try to talk to me and spoil the memory of our past ideal friendship. This is my only humble request to you.

—Vasantha

Vasantha left the letter on the table and went away. He was very hurt that a friend he had loved more than life itself had turned out to be of bad character. Without thinking twice, he wrote the letter and left.

It was not easy though to throw away a friendship that had taken root in his heart, not as easy as leaving. Though he convinced himself that what he had done was right, somewhere inside, a small voice kept pricking him, "You were wrong."

He went to the cinema with some friends in the evening. But unable to sit still until the film ended, he left midway and walked straight back, only realizing he was at the hostel when he saw the light on in Mahesha's room. He looked at the room with a sense of yearning and left. After walking around here and there, by the time he went back home, it was past ten o'clock. When he walked in, he found his little sister, Nalini, still awake. "Anna, Mahesha left a letter for you. I have kept it in your room," she said.

Mahesha's letter! Ignoring his mother who was telling him to come have dinner, he closed the door to his room and began reading.

Vasantha,

I got your letter this morning. I never thought that you would say such words. That was why I was immobile after reading your letter. After that, though I saw you packing your things, I could not say anything. I don't know what you must have thought seeing me remain silent. Maybe your suspicions became stronger.

I have been thinking about this since this morning. I don't think of it as an issue I cannot tell you about. Come to think of it, it is not a topic that I have to hide from anyone either. But look, Vasantha, when it is something that we think of as very important, we feel very bad when someone else says, "that's it?", if they get to know, and make light of it. That is why I hesitate to talk openly in front of people who don't understand my feelings. After having been friends over the last few months, you surely know me at least a little now. The proof that I hold your good opinion in high regard is that I am writing to you about things that I have never told anyone else.

I have a younger sister, Vasantha. She was born on the day my mother died. Though I was only three or four years old then, I remember very well my mother lying in the lap of death, my little sister lying near her, screaming and screaming, my father, silent, crying without tears...

Vasantha, you might ask, why all this now. If you have to understand the depth of love between me and Paapa (my little sister's pet name), if you have to know why I love her more than my elder sister Prabhe, I have to tell you about how our mother died the day she was born.

She was only a tiny baby then, she couldn't play with me, still I loved her so much. As we grew older, our bond became stronger. Prabha and I used to fight. But Paapa and I never ever fought. Prabhe is now married and living with her husband. The year she got married, our father remarried. Paapa must be nineteen or twenty years old now. She was not even eleven when she was married off to our aunt's son who had lost both his parents. The Sarda Bill had not yet been passed when she got married. She was married off in a hurry. A girl who was at an age to play was thrust upon that man, and our father agreed to give him money to go abroad to study. The year they got married, he passed matriculation. Our father bore the burden of financing his college education also. The year he finished BA he went away to Oxford aiming for an MA. When he went, my sister was fifteen years old. It was also the height of Satyagraha. It was a time when every individual was ready to sacrifice everything for the sake of the nation. Though she was not capable of fully understanding the political situation then, it was my sister's wish that her husband should not go abroad, that too to England. She could not say exactly why he ought not to go abroad. But still, she did not want him to go to England. He came home before he left for England. I don't know what exactly happened; she did not tell me. I am only guessing that she begged him not to go. I had a reason to guess this. Paapa had not spoken a word to him after they got married. I have already written that she had not completed even eleven years when the wedding took place. She thought that a husband is a thing to be shy of, and that if he came, she had to go and hide. He visited once a year for one or two days, Paapa would not even go in front of him. When he came home, seeing her go into his room by herself, I guessed that she went to request him not to go abroad. I don't know what he said. He walked away. When he left, she did not come out like we expected. I went to call her but her room was locked. I could hear her sobbing softly inside. I did not feel like telling her to come out just then. I went out. Her husband was ready to leave. Except for Paapa, all the members of the family were there. It did not seem like he noticed her absence; he left.

I did not see Paapa all that day. Father asked a couple of times, "Where is Paapa?" Our stepmother said, "She must be in her room." That was it...

Vasantha, this happened four years ago. Paapa was then an innocent girl who did not know anything. Not knowing maternal love or a mother's friendship, she was just a naughty girl who grew up like a tomboy with me. She was stubborn and insisted on doing what she was told not to do. There are only four-five years between then and now, Vasantha; but so much has happened in these years! The Paapa who was with me from childhood is no more...her husband killed her when he left to go abroad.

For about one or two months after he left, I thought one day or another she would feel better. But I turned out to be wrong. With every passing day Paapa, my motherless little sister Paapa, shrank. Seeing her in that state, father said, "It must be some illness, we should take her to a doctor." Our stepmother grumbled, "If she just sits in one place reading, what else can you expect?" Only I knew that Paapa did not have any physical illness. But why she should grieve so much if her husband went abroad for higher studies was a big question for me. I did not want to ask her about it. It was her nature to tell me everything without hesitation. She was pining so much, and yet had not confided anything in me, so I thought it best to not force her to talk to me. I decided not to ask until she herself was ready to tell me. I saw her shrink before my eyes with every passing day, but my decision remained unchanged.

Paapa wrote one or two letters to him. Not one got a reply. After seeing his lack of care, I strongly believed that he was the reason for Paapa's heartache. Even then, Paapa did not say anything. Her laughter, which used to light up the whole house, had disappeared somewhere. She would keep to herself, always in her room. Our old life that was filled with laughter, happiness and enthusiasm went away.

Somehow two years passed. Vasantha, those two years were as long as two eons for me. Finally, Paapa's husband passed in a high class and came back to the country. That day was a very happy, joyous day for all of us; even Paapa wore a faint smile. We got to know that he was going to come by that morning's train. Our father and

I went to the station to receive him, but he did not come. When we returned, disappointed, Paapa was standing by the door, looking out at the road. Seeing us both return without him, her face wilted even more. Her smile that had formed like sunshine in monsoon, disappeared. Pretending not to have seen that, I said, "Perhaps he missed the train; he will come tomorrow," to console her. Tomorrow came. Several tomorrows went by and one or two weeks passed. He did not come, neither did his letter.

About two weeks later, I opened the newspaper and found his photo! Below that it said, "After studying at Oxford University for two years, having passed in first class, Shri Rama Rao who has returned to India...has been appointed as a professor at University. Our congratulations to him." There were other words praising him further. It was natural that I would see this photo and be happy that my sister's husband had got a good job. But, Vasantha, for some reason, seeing his face in that photo made me very angry. Our father was the reason for his success. Our father was the one who gave him money and helped him study further. After all that, not a single letter to us after he returned to the country! He could have at least written a line to Paapa. Every time I saw Paapa who was expecting him to come tomorrow, tomorrow, I got angry at him. Though our father was hurting inside, in front of Paapa he used to say, "He must be very busy with work. That is why he did not have time to come or to write. He will come, surely, very soon..." This way, two–three months went by looking forward to him coming. Finally, our father wrote him a letter that said, "All these days, your studies were going on. Now after finishing all that, you have earned a job. At least now, come as soon as possible and take Paapa with you."

After one–two weeks, a reply from him arrived... "I don't have time to come now. I will try to come in the next vacation." That's all. Father read the letter and gave it to me. I also read it. I had not expected anything more from him. But our father...that letter acted like an electric shock on him. Even when our mother died, his face had not looked like that. He had raised the orphan and made him a human. He had honoured him by giving his daughter to him. Not even in his dreams had he thought that this would be the thanks he would get. Now…?

I had never thought of Paapa and cried before; but that day, I sobbed uncontrollably like a small child. I slapped my head repeatedly. I thought I would kill her husband. If I think of it now, I still feel the same.

Paapa saw the letter. She did not cry like we thought she would. She did not show that she was hurt in any way. Seeing her calmness, I felt ashamed and calmed myself. But I had a fear inside me: what if Paapa tried to kill herself? My guess was wrong in this regard. Seeing me not leaving her alone, she asked, "Anna, are you afraid that I will jump into some well?" and laughed dryly. "Nothing like that, Paapa…if you are alone, you will sit and worry, and feel hurt," I stammered. "What is the use of feeling hurt? If there was any point in it, these two years that you were pining…, did you know that something like this would happen, Paapa?" I questioned her. Paapa told me then what she had not shared for two years.

Vasantha, like I had guessed, Paapa had requested him not to go abroad that day. After all, he was also young. If he had insisted that he wanted to go, she would not have been that sad. But the things he said! "I got married to you only because I wanted to go to England. Otherwise, who would marry you?" Those words killed Paapa. Those words made her shrink and suffer for two years. If she had told us this earlier… but she did not say anything. She was not the sort of girl to talk about it. Paapa was the only one suffering for the last two years, thinking about those words. Now, everyone in our family was suffering. Though she was a bit gruff natured, our stepmother loved Paapa very much. She was very angry at Paapa's husband's behaviour.

The whole town knew that Paapa's husband had come back and that he had got a job. Our neighbours were very curious to know why Paapa had still not gone to her husband's house and started her marital life. Every day, they would question our stepmother regarding this and she would seethe in anger. It seems like even Paapa's friends would keep asking her. She would hesitate to come out of her room if her friends came around. Whether there is a reason or not...in our society, a wife who is rejected by her husband invites suspicion. Society's long tongue did not keep from criticizing Paapa.

It had been eight–nine months since he got the job. One evening when I came home, Paapa was sitting in my room. It was rare that she would come to my room in the evening. Wondering what this new thing was, I asked, "What is it, Paapa?" The lamp had not yet been lit. Though it was not pitch dark, I still could not see her face clearly in the dim light. But I could tell from her voice that she had cried a lot. I sat next to her, held her hands and said, "What is the use of crying, Paapa? You will only spoil your health, that's all. That creature is not worth even a single teardrop," trying to console her thus. Instead of feeling better, she began to cry even louder. Between sobs, she said, "Anna, you only take me and leave me there."

To push Paapa towards him because of her insistence! Though he did not want her, she was not any burden to us. Her words were a big surprise to me, they also made me angry. How can we deliberately push Paapa into hell! But Paapa would not listen to anything I said. She was stubborn about going, and though father, me, even our stepmother, were all against this, it was her stubbornness that won in the end. It fell on me to take her to his house.

Vasantha, even when the husband is a good man and the wife is the queen of his home, parents feel bad about sending daughters to their in-laws' houses. Now, to forcibly send Paapa, the light of our house, to a place where she was not wanted, do I have to say how sad we all were? All the members of the family came to the station, as if mourners after a death. How can I forget that day, Vasantha? Eyes overflowing with tears, my little sister looked at father standing at the station, until she could no longer see him. After he was too far to see, she went to a corner and sat down. Until our destination arrived, she did not speak a word. I also did not try to talk to her.

That town came, Vasantha. We got down from the train, hired a car and left for his house. Though we had informed him that we were coming, he had not come to the station. Neither had we expected him to come. That was a Sunday—he had the day off. It must have been around ten o'clock when we got there. He was lying in an easy-chair in the front hall and was flipping through the previous day's newspaper. "God is in his heaven and all is right with world" was what his appearance seemed to say. I was so angry that I wanted to kick him where he was lying, but I looked at Paapa's face and swallowed my anger.

Though he saw Paapa near the door, he pretended not to have seen her and, staying where he was, asked, "How are you, Mahesha?" Suppressing the anger that was rising in me, I said, "I have brought your wife with me." "What was the hurry for that? I had written that I would come in the vacation, didn't I?" he asked. "Two-three vacations have passed and you didn't come. Paapa is not a burden to us. We were not in any hurry to send her, but we couldn't bear her stubbornness, that is why I came. It is your responsibility to look after her now," I said and gave her to that animal.

He was quiet for a while after hearing my words. Then, "Sit down, Mahesha, I have to talk to you. If you hadn't hurried this so much, I would have come there and explained all this," he said. Till then, both Paapa and I were standing. He remained reclining. When he asked me to sit down, I called Paapa who was standing near the door and said, "Come, sit here." She did not come, and remained standing there.

Ignoring her, he said, "Look, Mahesha, I was a young boy when I married your sister. I couldn't ignore my maternal uncle's words and had to marry her. I did not know my own mind then. See now, I have become an individual; I also have intelligence and an ego. Why should I spoil my whole life for something that happened when I was too young to be aware of anything? A forced wedding somehow took place long ago. There is nothing to be done now. I have come to a decision now. Let your sister be in your house only. I am ready to give money for her expenses. What more can I say?"

The anger I had suppressed till then erupted now. "I did not bring Paapa here because we cannot afford to look after her. If you don't want her, she also does not want the money you are earning from the education you gained because of her," I said, telling Paapa, "Come, Paapa, what other work do we have here?" and started walking away. He also did not stop us. Maybe he was happy that he had won so easily. Paapa did not move from the door. I went up to her, took her hand and said, "Come, you are not a burden to us. Come, let's go." Paapa removed her hand from mine and went to him. Bathing his feet in her tears, she said, "If you don't want me as your wife, give me some space to stay here at least as your servant," she begged. Maybe his heart would have melted at her request. But just then, a young woman, wearing a modern dress and with a tennis racquet in her hand, walked in with a natural confidence. Having come from the bright light outside, it did not seem like she had noticed the two of us. Seeing her, he struggled to get up from the easy-chair. Paapa also stood up. Then she saw me and Paapa. Her surprised look at him contained a question: "who are they?" After having insulted my sister, he turned to me, held the woman's hand and said, "Mahesha, this is my wife, Malathi." Paapa, who had been standing there like a statue ever since the woman had walked in, heard his words and walked out without looking back at him. I also followed her without saying another word to him.

It's been two–three years since all this happened. Initially, we had lost hope regarding Paapa. Vasantha, even the doctor had said that she wouldn't live. But still in the end she lived. Her health im-proved too. However, the smile that was always dancing on her face said, "I will never ever return", and went away. My sister is not a beauty, Vasantha, she is like everyone else. But in intelligence, good manners and behaviour, rare are those that can match her. To make sure we all don't feel sad because of her, she swallowed her pain and went about the house. After that day I have never seen her cry again.

The grief at the state Paapa was in, like a widow though she had a husband, made our father follow our mother within one year of all this happening. Within another one month of that, our stepmother, already a heart patient, followed him in death. The ones who were left, me and Paapa, Paapa and me.

Around the same time, we suffered financially as well. The house and the fields had to be sold to cover the loans we had taken to finance Paapa's husband's education abroad. The only thing left was the BA degree I received that year. If my father was alive, I would have joined medical college. After his death, the thirst for studying lay discarded in a corner and only the thirst for filling our stomachs remained. Vasantha, when I think of Paapa's patience, calmness and strength to work for me without thinking of herself during those days, it still surprises me, and I wonder where my little sister was hiding this kind of strength.

There is a proverb, Vasantha, "get ruined and join the city." We had decided to leave our town. There was nothing there to call our own. Also, why did we have to live in a place where people commented on Paapa's status constantly? The day before we were to leave, there was a public function in town. After packing the few things, we had, not having anything else to do, we went to this function. The girl who was to sing "Vande Mataram" had not come for some reason. Our Paapa sings very well. The secretary of that function knew this and he asked Paapa to sing. She could not say no. That day when she sang "Vande Mataram", the entire audience was stunned. Her voice was that good, the way she sang, that attractive way in which she sang…and, the song was Vande Mataram, after all.

Vasantha, that day's 'Vande Mataram' changed my sister's life entirely. Two–three years ago, she was the Paapa who had been rejected by her husband. Now! Now she is the famous film star Miss Aruna Devi! There is no one in the whole country who has not heard her heavenly music, who has not seen her unique acting. From the point of view of the world, how happy she is. Vasantha, I am the only person who knows that she has neither happiness, nor peace. Her only happiness is my education now. Though I don't have a wish to study with her money, no word of mine works before her stubbornness.

Vasantha, for people, the Paapa who was rejected by her first husband is now a film star. A film star! Do people need anything more than this to call her perverse, immoral?

Vasantha, the girl you saw with me is my sister Paapa. Let people say anything they want about me and her, it does not bother us. But you...please don't look at us the way other people do. I don't wish for anything else from you apart from this, Vasantha. Except for you and Paapa, there is no one in this world I can call my own. I cannot bear it if you also have a wrong opinion of me. That is why I have written to you about these things that I hesitate to tell anyone. If, after reading this, your opinion of me still does not change, then let this be my last salutation to you....

Mahesha

Not caring that it was midnight, Vasantha ran to Mahesha's room with the tear-soaked letter in his hand.

The Day Before

Note: *This is part of the story Gouramma was working on the day before she went swimming and her journey on earth ended. Kaada is our mestri, the estate supervisor. He is still with us as our mestri. These are just two chapters from his life. This story ends here. Gouramma's too.*

—B.T. Gopalakrishna (Gouramma's husband)

* * *

If Mahatma Gandhi preached Hindu-Muslim unity, Kaada mestri was the one who actually practised it. His is a strange story.

By birth he belonged to a community of oil millers. He lost his father when he was nine years old. His mother remarried. Till he was ten, he somehow lived in that house even though he did not find it comfortable in his stepfather's house. One day he left without telling anyone. Having borne children from her second marriage, his mother did not attempt to look for him. What will the stepfather care? Thinking that it is good that the evil went out of the house, he kept quiet.

The little boy, just ten years old. There was no reason to wonder what he would do in the wide world. Having grown up on his mother's milk and in the lap of adversity, he had no fears at all. If he did even half the work that he used to do in his step father's house, he would get plenty of food. Apart from having enough rice to fill his belly, he did not have any other desire. For a month or two, he roamed around, worked in different houses and filled his belly.

Then one day, he went to a coffee plantation. Who would refuse a labourer who won't ask for loans and will work for a fistful of food? Mestri Jinraju added him to the roster and got him started on work at the plantation from the very next day. This way two more months passed by. During this time, the owner of the plantation bought a pair of Alsatian dogs. He needed a smart boy to look after them. Dore (European planters in coffee plantations were called Dore, meaning master) told Jinraju mestri to send a suitable boy. The mestri had come to appreciate Kaada's work over the last two months ago. The Dore also saw him and approved. From the next day, Kaada became the boy who looked after the dogs in the Dore's bungalow. This was the first chapter of Kaada's life.

The Dore greatly loved dogs. He had to see them at all times of the day. Because of them, his attention would occasionally fall on Kaada too. His activities, diligence, and polite behaviour, helped gain him the Dore's love. As a result of this love, Kaada was liberated from looking after the dogs and was made the Dore's personal attendant. The Dore's love did not stop there; it got him to get Kaada converted to Christianity as well. After all, Kaada was a boy of eleven. He had grown up thinking that one is born to work and to fill one's belly without any knowledge of religion. What did he know about how one must not reject one's religion and convert to another? So what if it is any religion? So what if it is any creed? A stomach full of food, clothes to cover his body, plus two rupees salary every month—when he has all this, why worry about religion or creed? Also, is it a surprise that when the Dore told him to convert to his religion, poor Kaada was very happy? Is it any small privilege to join the Dore's religion? Kaada became a Christian and was named Joseph Kaada. That was not the only privilege Kaada had as the Dore's personal servant. He learnt to speak a little bit of English too by speaking with the Dore who did not know Kannada,

Now Kaada was not the Kaada of one year ago, when he was weak with hunger. Full of poise and style now, his own mother would not have been able to recognize him if she saw him.

This way, Kaada spent the next seven–eight years without any difficulties. Then, due to financial constraints, the Dore sold the plantation and went abroad. But before he left, he made sure to recommend Kaada's work to the new owner. The person who had bought the plantation had some other plantations as well. That was why, instead of coming to live there, he appointed a manager. As per the old Dore's recommendation, Kaada got the job of looking after the manager's horse. Apart from grooming the horse, he also went twice a day to the village three miles away to bring the post.

While going to the village to collect the post, the manager would sometimes tell Kaada to ride the horse so that it would get some exercise. On the way to the village there was a small petty shop owned by a Mappila Muslim. The owner Mummu Kaka did not have much business and used to also work as a mestri and supply labourers. He had to sometimes go to the neighbouring Dakshin Kannada district to bring labourers. During those times his sister, Hussain Bibi, used to sit in the shop and manage the business. Their old mother did not know how to keep accounts. Hussain Bibi was smart in her work. She was an expert in accounts, business and trade. To top it, she was slim, fair and beautiful. When the sister Hussain Bibi sat in the shop, there would be more business than when the brother Mummu Kaka managed the shop. Mestris and labourers from the plantations nearby would come to her shop to buy beedis, tobacco leaves, betel leaves, areca nut, soda and other things.

While he had no addictive habits when he lived only within the plantation, Kaada had developed the habit of smoking beedis when he started going to the village every day. Initially, Kaada would buy beedis from the village. One day, he had used up all the beedis. Since he had to smoke on the way, he went to the roadside shop. That day Hussainbi was managing the shop. He gave one anna and bought a pack of beedis. Hussainbi used to always see Kaada riding to the village and back on top of a horse as tall as a mountain. Those from the other plantations used to go on foot to collect the post, and since he was the only one going atop a horse, she thought he must be better than them. That he never used to come to her shop increased her estimation of him. Since he had grown up in the Dore's house, his clothes were also cleaner and of a different style than those of other mestris and plantation workers. The Dore's old hat and his broken English had helped to elevate him from the ordinary labour force to a higher level. Crowning all this was his smiling face. It was thus no surprise that he looked extraordinary to Hussainbi.

She was very happy seeing him come to her shop. With a smile on her face, she gave him the pack of beedis and asked, "What else do you want?"

Focussing only on the beedi, Kaada placed one in his mouth and put his hand into his pocket for a matchbox, but found none. She gave him one. He lit the beedi, put the matchbox in his pocket and turned to leave. She asked, "Money for the matchbox?"

Lost in the beedi, he had forgotten to pay for the matchbox. When she asked, "I had forgotten; I will pay," he said and turned back.

She was standing there saying, "It is okay." While handing over the money, Kaada saw her.

From that day onwards, Kaada never bought a beedi in the village again. Now if Kaada wanted beedis, it was from Hussainbi's shop. Why only if he needed beedis? Even if he didn't want them, he would use it as an excuse and go there. But when Mummu Kaka was in the shop, Kaada did not want many beedis. This way, by the time six months passed, Kaada felt that he could not live without beedis, and Hussainbi who sold those beedis. Hussainbi too, while selling beedis to Kaada every day, gave away her heart. Mummu Kaka got to know via their old mother about the love that was growing in the garb of beedis. He had only one younger sister. He had brought her up with much love. He did not wish to stand in the way of her happiness. Kaada was also a worthy groom. Young. Not arrogant. He had worked in the same place for many years honestly and saved some money too. His sister loved him too. But...? The issue of religion stood in the way like a mountain.

One day he himself broached the subject with Kaada. What did Kaada care? In his eyes, religion had no importance. With more enthusiasm than he had shown on becoming a Christian, he agreed to be a Muslim. Before this he had left his religion for a handful of food, but love was the reason now. He was ready to give up his life for Hussainbi. It did not take him long to convert to Islam when he realized that he could marry her if he gave up a religion that he had no value for. Maybe if his old Dore was around, there might have been a problem! But the current manager, who was a Hindu, kept quiet thinking what did he care if the Christian Kaada became a Muslim. Thus, for the sake of love Kaada converted a second time, became Ismail Kaada Kaka and did nikah with Hussainbi.

This was the second chapter of Kaada's life.

About the Author and Translator

Kodagina Gouramma (1912–1939) was one of the three major women writers in Kannada of the early 20th century, and among the first to explore feminist themes in her works. A nationalist, a freedom fighter, as also a budding politician, Gouramma was born and raised in Madikeri in Kodagu, a district famous for its coffee production in Karnataka state. Her career was barely over half a decade and twenty-one short stories old when she died in a swimming accident at the age of twenty-seven.

Deepa Bhasthi is a writer and translator. Her essays, columns and journalism has been widely published nationally and internationally. Her debut work of translation from the Kannada, Dr Kota Shivarama Karanth's 'The Same Village, The Same Tree' was published by Kuvempu Bhasha Bharathi Pradhikara in August 2022. She lives on a farm in Madikeri, Kodagu with her husband and two dogs.